Kim Rennie

UNDERGROUND AND OVERGROUND TRAINS

Capital Transport

Photographs are by the author except:

Capital Transport: cover and pages 2, 7 bottom, 13, 17, 19, 21, 23, 26, 27, 28, 32, 35, 49.
Justin Bailey: pages 1, 7 top, 12 top, 16, 24, 53, 68, 69 top.
Brian Hardy: pages 25, 60 top.
Mark Kehoe: 36, 69 bottom.
Colin Marsden: 51, 65, 66, 67.
George Odlum: 60 bottom.

ISBN 978-1-85414-417-1

Published by Capital Transport Publishing Ltd
www.capitaltransport.com

Printed in the EU

CONTENTS

Title page Contrasts in profiles: (Top) Bakerloo Line 1972 Mk II Tube Stock and London Overground Class 378/2 unit; (Bottom) Metropolitan Line S8 Stock and Piccadilly Line 1973 Tube Stock.

AUTHOR'S NOTE

This book describes and illustrates the rolling stock that runs on London Underground, London Overground and TfL Rail. Over the past ten years or so, there have been many changes. The Waterloo & City Line has seen its 1992 Tube Stock trains refurbished, whilst the Jubilee Line gained a capacity increase by the addition of a seventh car within the existing 1996 Tube Stock fleet, plus had four extra trains built. The Victoria Line's 1967 Tube Stock has all been replaced by 2009 Tube Stock; and on the Sub-Surface lines the introduction of S Stock has enabled the entire A Stock, C Stock and D Stock fleets to be withdrawn. A programme of 'refreshing' trains, both internally and externally, has been carried out on the Northern Line, is now underway on the Jubilee Line and is planned for the Central Line. In addition, the 1972 Tube Stock is undergoing life-extension work at Acton Works.

The engineers' train fleet has seen the majority of battery locomotives modernised and a number of the Schöma diesels converted to battery/electric operation. New tamping machines have entered service and orders placed in China to replace the majority of the existing wagons.

London Overground (LO) extended its operations in 2015 to take over the Lea Valley Lines and the Romford – Upminster shuttle, leading to ex-BR Class 315 and 317 trains entering their fleet. At the same time, TfL Rail was launched to assume control of the Liverpool Street – Shenfield service and they acquired the remainder of the Class 315 units. New Class 345 and 710 trains have been ordered and are due to enter service in 2017 and 2018 respectively.

Thanks and acknowledgments are due to Andrew Emmerson and Brian Hardy, who together provided the nucleus of the current text and the inspiration for its updating; and to Brian especially for providing historical and technical assistance, as well as checking the facts. The London Underground Railway Society (lurs.org.uk) publishes regular rolling stock information in its monthly magazine *Underground News* and enables readers to keep the information in this book up to date.

Kim Rennie

Opposite From the fleet of London Underground engineers' trains two modernised TransPlant battery locomotives pass through West Kensington, having just exited Lillie Bridge depot. They will use the crossover just beyond the far end of the platform to access the westbound District Line track as part of their return trip to Ruislip depot.

ABBREVIATIONS

BREL	BREL Ltd, Derby and York (later ABB Transportation Ltd).
Bombardier	Bombardier Prorail Ltd, Horbury, Wakefield (later Bombardier Transportation UK).
Cravens	Cravens Ltd, Sheffield.
Metro-Cammell	Metropolitan-Cammell Carriage & Wagon Company Ltd, Birmingham (later Alsthom, now Alstom).
Schöma	Schöma Locomotiven, Diepholz, Germany.
4LM	Four Lines Modernisation Project
AC	Alternating Current
ATO	Automatic Train Operation
ATP	Automatic Train Protection
AWS	Automatic Warning System
BR	British Railways / British Rail
CBTC	Communications Based Train Control
CCTV	Closed Circuit Television
CTC	Certificate of Technical Conformance
DC	Direct Current
DM	Driving Motor car
DMS	Driving Motor Standard
DMSO	Driving Motor Standard Open
DMU	Diesel Multiple Unit

DOO	Driver-Only Operation
DSD	Driver's Safety Device
DTCO	Driving Trailer Composite Open
DTSO	Driving Trailer Standard Open
ELL	East London Line
EMU	Electrical Multiple Unit
ETCS	European Train Control System
GEC	General Electric Company
IGBT	Insulated Gate Bipolar Transistor
JLE	Jubilee Line Extension
LCD	Liquid Crystal Display
LED	Light Emitting Diode
LER	London Electric Railway
LMS	London, Midland & Scottish Railway
LNER	London & North Eastern Railway
LO	London Overground
LT	London Transport
LU	London Underground
MS	Motor Shoe car
MSO	Motor Standard Open
NDM	Non-Driving Motor car
NLL	North London Line
NSE	Network SouthEast
OPO	One-Person Operation
PDC	Passenger Door Control
PMSO	Pantograph Motor Standard Open
PTSO	Pantograph Trailer Standard Open
RAT	Rail Adhesion Train
ROSCO	Rolling Stock Operating Company
ST	Special Trailer car
T	Trailer car
TBTC	Transmission Based Train Control
TCO	Trailer Composite Open
TfL	Transport for London
TOC	Train Operating Company
TOPS	Total Operations Processing System
TPWS	Train Protection and Warning System
TRV	Track Recording Vehicle
TSO	Trailer Standard Open
UNDM	Uncoupling Non-Driving Motor car
WLL	West London Line

UNDERGROUND TUBE STOCK TRAINS

1972 TUBE STOCK (Bakerloo Line)

The 1972 Tube Stock comprises the oldest trains in service on London Underground. The design was an adaption of the Victoria Line's 1967 Tube Stock, but modified for crew operation using a motorman and guard and formed of seven-cars instead of eight. The trains were equipped for manual driving under conventional signalling as opposed to Automatic Train Operation (ATO). At that time, it was felt desirable for ATO trains to operate without traditional side cab doors and the 1972 Tube Stock continued to omit this feature. This caused problems during peak hour crew reliefs at tunnel stations when the driver had to negotiate a crowded car saloon and led to step-plates and horizontal handrails being fitted to cab fronts. The step-plates were later removed, both in the interests of health and safety and because they became increasingly unnecessary following the closure of most of the inner London train crew booking-on and meal relief points in the 1980s.

Thirty trains (later referred to as 1972 MkI) were built for use on the Northern Line by Metro-Cammell at Birmingham to allow the worst examples of 1938 Tube Stock to be withdrawn. The latter were becoming increasingly unreliable, hence the decision to adapt the 1967 Tube Stock design rather than develop a completely new train. The initial order comprised 90 driving motor cars (DM), 90 trailers (T) and 30 uncoupling non-driving motor cars (UNDM), all in unpainted aluminium with black roofs and with red block

UNDERGROUND fleetnames on DM cars instead of the traditional London Transport script. Trains were formed into three- or four-car units, one of each being required to form a complete train as DM–T–T–M+UNDM–T–DM (or reverse). One four-car unit is now formed as DM–T–T–UNDM. The first train entered service on the Northern Line on 26 June 1972 and all 30 were in use by June 1973. Some of these cars were later converted to run on the Victoria Line formed within the existing 1967 Tube Stock fleet to provide increased capacity, whilst others were modified to augment services on the Bakerloo Line.

The second batch of 1972 Tube Stock (referred to as 1972 MkII) were intended for eventual use on the Fleet Line, but were initially used on the Northern Line, allowing further examples of the 1938 Tube Stock to be replaced. The 1972 MkII order was for 33 trains, also placed with Metro-Cammell, and comprised 99 driving motor cars, 99 trailers and 33 uncoupling non-driving motor cars. The first of these entered service in November 1973 and were generally similar in appearance to their MkI predecessors. Visible differences included Bus Red passenger doors and a plain red LT roundel on all car sides. Passive-provision for ATO in the future was provided with the MkII trains being fitted with 'calling on' lights and Allen West 'tiller' door controllers in cabs. Although the MkI and MkII units were not compatible when delivered, subsequent modifications enabled them to run together.

Opposite Bakerloo Line trains run on Network Rail tracks north of Queen's Park and are shared with London Overground's Euston – Watford services. 'D'-end DM car 3550 leads at Stonebridge Park on a service to Harrow & Wealdstone. These are now the last LU trains to use roller destination blinds.

Opposite Externally, the 1972 Mk II Tube Stock are almost identical to the earlier Victoria Line 1967 Tube Stock from which they were developed. This is trailer car 4256.

The interiors of both batches followed those of the 1967 Tube Stock in being predominantly grey with colour relief provided by the seat moquette, and in DM cars a red melamine-finished 'J'-door leading to the cab. MkI cars continued with the red/black/grey moquette pattern used on the 1967 Stock whilst MkIIs featured a blue/green design as used on contemporary LT buses. All cars had the traditional Underground varnished grooved maple wood floors.

Car bodies are formed of welded steel underframes and aluminium alloy panelling. DM cars have two double doors and one single door per side, whilst T and UNDM cars have two double doors and two single per side, in all cases being of the traditional internal-sliding design. Seating is 36 longitudinal each in T cars and 40 combined longitudinal and transverse each in DM and UNDM cars, making a total of 268 on a seven-car train.

DM and UNDM cars are fitted with automatic Wedgelock couplers at outer ends (mechanical only on 35XX DMs), with individual cars bar-coupled within units. Service braking is achieved through a combination of rheostatic and electro-pneumatic brakes (EP), and EP and Westinghouse brakes in emergency. Train protection is by conventional trip-cock/trainstop and deadman's handle. Eleven trailer cars are equipped with de-icing equipment.

From 1977, in a complex series of inter-line transfers, new 1973 Tube Stock delivered to the Piccadilly Line allowed the 1956/59 Tube Stock to be displaced to the Northern Line. This then released the 1972 MkII Tube Stock for transfer to the Bakerloo in readiness for the Stanmore branch becoming part of the Jubilee Line (as the Fleet Line had been renamed). The process was a gradual one but completed in time for the opening of the Jubilee Line between Stanmore and Charing Cross on 1 May 1979. In the interim period, the 1972 MkII Tube Stock worked on all parts of the Bakerloo Line, including as far as Watford Junction and into Croxley depot. Four MkII trains were returned to the Northern Line during 1983 and subsequently a further 14 trains followed.

In 1984 and 1985, the delivery of new 1983 Tube Stock for the Jubilee allowed the 1972 MkII Tube Stock to be moved to the Bakerloo Line and this was fully achieved by March 1989. These trains were subsequently sent to Acton Works for conversion to OPO, with guard's panels removed from the saloon and door controls relocated in the driving cab; and this mode of working commenced on the Bakerloo Line from 20 November 1989.

Between 1991 and 1995 the trains were refurbished by Tickford Rail at Rosyth Royal Dockyard. The most obvious change was the application of corporate LU red, white and blue livery. Internally, brighter off-white finishes replaced shades of grey and unpainted grab poles were changed to a line-themed brown. The wooden floors were also removed, being replaced by fire-resistant rubber material. Other alterations were a new seat moquette pattern, the installation of a digitised voice announcement (DVA) system for passenger information, and an audible 'doors closing' warning system. Traditional 'ball' straphangers were by replaced by handrails, a policy applied to

The 'refreshed' interior of a 1972 Mk II Tube Stock car showing the special brown version of the Barman seat moquette and the new floor covering including colour-contrasting areas at doorways. Retained are the brown line-themed grab poles dating from the 1990s. The 1972 Tube stock is now the only Tube-profile train to offer transverse seating bays.

The internal refit did not reinstate conventional seat armrests but rather continued with the provision of small padded 'dividers'. Note the traditional LT roundel 'No Smoking' signs which are now unique to the Bakerloo Line.

all future rolling stock refurbishments. Not continued was the use of roller destination blinds and these are now the last LU trains to retain them. The lettering on these is now in upper and lower case rather than all in capitals.

26 MkI cars were converted for use on the Bakerloo Line and reclassified as MkIIs, where they help form a combined fleet of 36 x seven-car trains. All of the 1972 Tube Stock are now showing their age, cosmetically, structurally and in reliability, and are overdue for replacement. This is unlikely to take place until 2026 at the earliest, so in January 2014 a life-extension programme began in Acton Works. This includes corrosion and weld repairs and the fitting of Rail Vehicle Accessibility Requirement (RVAR)-compliant flooring. Future work will include the provision of two wheelchair bays in a single car on each seven-car train and associated external signage. Other changes will be to handrails and passenger emergency alarms, improved passenger information systems and the installation of LED lighting. In a separate programme, a special brown version of the corporate 'Barman' seat moquette has been designed and is now fitted to all trains.

One four-car unit of 1972 MkI Tube stock, comprising cars 3229-4229-4329-3329, remains operational for filming and training purposes. The train is normally kept in the disused Aldwych branch platform at Holborn and is periodically worked to Northfields depot for maintenance. Livery is unpainted aluminium with all-red cab fronts.

1973 TUBE STOCK (Piccadilly Line)

Following the authorisation of the Piccadilly Line extension to Heathrow Airport in 1970, it was clear that new rolling stock including adequate space for luggage would be desirable. An order was placed with Metro-Cammell for 87½ six-car trains comprising 196 driving motor cars, 175 trailers and 154 uncoupling non-driving motor cars. Although the new cars would be around 6ft feet longer than on the existing rolling stock, the total length of a six-car train was about 17ft shorter than a seven-car 1938/56/59 Tube Stock train. This was because it was planned to convert the trains to OPO (then referred to as one man operation) at a later date and thus the passenger door controls were provided in driving cabs instead of on a traditional guard's gangway at the inner end of DM cars. When the guard operated the doors it was necessary for the rear cab to be fully within the platform, and similarly, when eventually in OPO mode, the front cab had to be within station limits in order to allow the safe control of the doors by the driver. The first train of 1973 Tube Stock entered service on 19 July 1975 as a passenger-carrying 'special' for the extension to Hatton Cross, followed on 15 August 1975 by the first normal passenger working.

An eastbound 1973 Tube Stock train arrives at Earl's Court on a service to Cockfosters.

Trains are formed of three-car units, the majority of which are formed DM-T-UNDM and UNDM-T-DM. In addition 21 'double-ended' units were formed as DM-T-DM to increase fleet flexibility, as they could then be used at either end of a six-car train. These formerly operated as three-car units on the Holborn – Aldwych shuttle, which is why an extra 'half' train was part of the original order. Four different coupling formations are possible – DM-T-UNDM+UNDM-T-DM, DM-T-DM+ UNDM-T-DM, DM-T-UNDM+DM-T-DM and DM-T-DM+DM-T-DM.

Livery as delivered was unpainted aluminium with a Bus Red half cab front and red LT roundels on all cars. Early units had roofs painted black but this was changed to white after the first 16 in an attempt to reduce internal temperatures. Interior décor was mostly light grey, though with colour provided by bright yellow car ends. Seat moquette was originally of the blue/grey pattern used on 1972 MkIIs and wood flooring continued to be fitted.

Construction was in many ways an evolution from the 1972 Tube Stock, with bodies formed of welded steel underframes and aluminium alloy panelling. DM cars have two double doors and one single door per side, whilst T and UNDM cars have two double doors and two single per side, again being of the internal-sliding design. The 1973 Tube Stock doors however had a 'stand back' area designed to accommodate airport passengers' luggage. Trains originally seated 264 passengers in either longitudinal or transverse form with 44 each in all cars.

Most DM cars are fitted with mechanical couplers only. Automatic Wedgelock couplers are provided on UNDMs and on the DMs of 'double-ended' units, as these are the only cars required to couple within a six-car train. Service and emergency braking is achieved through a combination of the rheostatic and Westcode systems and this was the first time the traditional Westinghouse brake had been omitted from an LT rolling stock design (following trials using a 1967 Tube Stock unit). Train protection is by conventional tripcock/ trainstop and deadman's handle.

Improvements incorporated in these trains included air-operated cab doors, operated independently of the passenger doors, and a 'selective door close' facility enabling all except one single door and one single leaf of a double door on each car to be closed, a useful facility in bad weather at terminal stations and during prolonged station stops, though rarely used nowadays. A fault-finding panel was provided in the cab for the driver to identify defects on the train. Also provided was automatic wheel-slip/slide protection and load control of acceleration and braking. A total of 25 single-ended 'A' units were fitted from new with de-icing equipment.

Sliding ventilators were provided above the car windows. The intention to fit three ceiling-mounted fans on each car was hampered by design and technical difficulties and it was not until October 1977 that fans were first used. Even so they were not wholly successful. Not all cars were fitted with fans and those that did have them were subsequently decommissioned.

The Piccadilly Line was the first of the deep-level Tube lines to be converted to one-person operation on 31 August 1987 (the Victoria Line having been in that mode from opening). The 1973 Tube Stock was modified for OPO between 1986 and 1987. Exterior differences included the fitting of an offside window wiper and a calling-on light (the original as-built calling-on lights having been removed to allow the installation of a cab ventilator).

Following an experimental conversion by Metro-Cammell in 1990, a contract for refurbishing the 1973 Tube Stock was awarded to RFS, soon absorbed into Bombardier Prorail, with work commencing in May 1993. Trains were refurbished internally and externally, including the application of corporate LU livery. To increase security, windows were fitted to trailing ends of cars allowing a view into the adjacent carriage. All seating became longitudinal, reducing capacity from 44 to 38 per car (228 in total). However, perch seats were provided at car ends and by the door area in the centre bay, enhancing luggage and standing space. The wooden floors were replaced by rubber and a new red/grey/black design of seat moquette provided in place of the original blue/green design. Bright yellow end panelling and other 1970s finishes were also supplanted by more subdued colours, whilst the grab poles became blue or yellow. Interior scrolling dot matrix indicators (DMI) and pre-set DVA messages were also fitted and the roller destination blinds were replaced by LCD displays. Train-to-track hinged steps with handrails were fitted as an integral part of cab fronts and, in conjunction with extra lighting, were designed to assist with emergency detrainments. The first refurbished train re-entered service on 17 June 1996, and the programme was completed in four years.

Changes in more recent years saw a common seat moquette pattern rolled out across the Jubilee, Northern and Piccadilly lines by Tube Lines. This featured a blue/black base colour with random red, orange and green squares of varying sizes. That on the first two lines has been replaced by the new blue-based standard LU 'Barman' design and the Piccadilly is expected to follow suit. A more recent development is the provision of two Piccadilly Line Rail Adhesion Trains. Two 'double-ended' 1973 Tube Stock units were temporarily taken out of service in 2017 and each fitted with a removable pallet containing a Sandite dispensing module. These are designed to operate as three-car trains between Arnos Grove and Cockfosters, and Northfields to Osterley, during the leaf-fall season.

The current 1973 Tube Stock fleet consists of 86 trains – six cars have been scrapped, two are in store and one is now in the Track Recording Train. Replacement is scheduled for 2023-25 under the Deep Tube Upgrade Programme.

The Central Line's 1992 Tube Stock was 'refreshed' just prior to the 2012 London Olympics. Visible changes included strengthened window surrounds and greater areas of red on the cab ends. This is a westbound train at Woodford.

1992 TUBE STOCK
(Central and Waterloo & City Lines)

Following trials with three prototype trains (the now withdrawn 1986 Tube Stock) an order for 85 trains of Central Line Replacement Stock (as it was then known) was placed in 1989 with BREL of Derby (later ABB Transportation). The outcome was a fleet of modern trains incorporating a number of new features such as electronic traction control and a fully integrated train control and management system.

Each train of 1992 Tube Stock comprises eight cars formed of four two-car units (two two-car units on the Waterloo & City Line). There are three combinations of 2-car unit and four types of individual vehicle. Car 'A' is a driving motor car (DM) with cab, collector shoes, traction equipment. Car 'B' is a non-driving motor car (NDM) having no cab or shoes, but has traction equipment fed from the adjacent motor car. It also has a shunting control cabinet at its outer end. Car type 'C' is similarly a non-driving motor car having no cab, but has shoes and traction equipment like an 'A' car, along with a shunting control cabinet at its outer end. De-icing cars are a variation on car type 'C' and are designated as type 'D'. With these four types of car, semi-permanent two-car units are formed as follows: 175 A-B units, 133 B-C units and 32 B-D de-icing units. All the two-car units are fully-reversible and compatible and thus there is no distinction between 'A' and 'D' ends as before. With the different combination of cars and units, it is possible for an 8-car train to be formed in one of 36 different ways, although DM cars are kept at the outer ends of trains whenever possible. Trains were delivered in LU corporate livery from new, the first rolling stock so treated, as have all subsequent LU passenger trains to date.

The bodyshells are made from welded extruded aluminium sections whereby the melted alloy is formed into cross-sections using bespoke moulds. Door provision is two double and one single per side on 'A' cars and two double and two single on 'B', 'C' and 'D' cars, in all cases externally-hung. The doors are wider than previously to allow speedier alighting and boarding and thereby reduce station stop times. Passenger door control buttons (PDC), both for opening and closing, were provided from new. Since early 2000, however, the train doors have been under control of the train operator.

Each car has all-longitudinal seating, arranged six per side in the outer bays and five per side in the centre saloon bay (i.e. between the double doors), giving a total of 34 seats per car (a total 272 for an eight-car train). The middle pair of each group of six is set back six inches to allow greater standing capacity, at which point there is a floor-to-ceiling grab pole in the centre. At non cab-fitted ends (i.e. at the trailing end of car 'A' and both ends of cars 'B', 'C' and 'D') there is one perch seat in each corner position. The large single-glazed car windows, which curve up into the roof line, have also been adopted from the prototype trains. Apart from the driving end of the 'A' cars, end windows are provided to give greater security. Interior finishes were mainly off-white with a red/blue square seat pattern and the colour contrast was provided by red-painted grab poles. In addition the traditional straphangers of earlier stocks were dispensed with in favour of ceiling handrails.

The functional interior of a 1992 Tube Stock car with seat moquette now changed to Barman blue. Seat 'perches' are situated either side of the end communicating doors and some longitudinal seats are set back to increase standing capacity.

Other interior features include pre-programmed announcements in digitised speech. The driver's cab incorporates in-cab CCTV which for the first time provided pictures of the relevant station platform, including views on departure. In addition to public address, in the event of an emergency, there is two-way communication between the driver and passengers. The driver was provided with a redesigned fore/aft traction brake controller which is positioned on the right hand side of the train operator's seat. For the first time a 'detrainment ramp' was fitted to DM car cab fronts to allow passengers to access the track in emergencies. These have since been removed as they were not regarded as being up to the job.

Automatic Wedgelock couplers are fitted to the outer ends of all units. Fully-blended dynamic regenerative rheostatic and EP braking with slip/slide protection is provided together with spring-applied parking brakes. The trains used LCD destination displays as first trailed on the experimental 1986 Tube Stock but these became very unreliable and at one point printed cards were displayed in cab windows instead. The LCD screens were subsequently replaced by LED equipment (as has also been done on the 1995 and 1996 Tube Stock). The exception is on the Waterloo & City Line where permanent printed labels show either 'Bank' or 'Waterloo'.

Three 1992 Tube Stock trains meet at North Acton. Trains can reverse in the middle platform, which was originally the eastbound line, prior to the commissioning of a new eastbound platform adjacent to the un-electrified Network Rail track in 1993.

The wide externally-hung doors on the 1992 Tube Stock are designed to speed up boarding and alighting times. PDC buttons are still fitted but are no longer in use.

Construction of the new trains began in 1990 and the first four cars were delivered to Ruislip depot on 17 May 1992. The first train entered passenger service on 7 April 1993. This introduced OPO to the Central Line 'main' for the first time, though it had previously been used on the Hainault – Woodford and Epping – Ongar shuttles using 1960 Tube Stock (and with 1967 Tube Stock on the former too). Sufficient trains were available for the full Monday to Friday service to be worked by 1992 Stock from Monday 20 February 1995, with the last 1962 Tube Stock having run on 17 February, thus ending the use of guards on the Central Line,

Train protection was initially by conventional tripcock/trainstop and dead-man's handle, but the first stage of Automatic Train Protection (ATP) commenced on the western branches on 19 June 1995, when trains ran in ATP from West Ruislip to Northolt. By 10 November 1997, the whole of the Central Line had been converted to ATP with manual

driving to target speeds and block marker boards as well as colour light signals. Full ATO was introduced between Wanstead and Gants Hill from 16 December 1999 and the entire line was so-equipped by May 2001.

Replacement rolling stock was also required on British Rail's Waterloo & City Line, which was then using ex-Southern Railway Class 487 units dating from 1940. There were replaced in 1993 by new Class 482 trains that were virtually identical to LU's 1992 Tube Stock, other than being finished in a version of Network SouthEast (NSE) livery, though without yellow cab fronts. Waterloo & City Line trains are composed of a pair of two-car units, each formed of an 'E' DM and an 'F' NDM that are, in most respects, almost identical to the A-B two-car units on the Central Line. The fleet comprised ten two-car units that were an 'add-on' order to London Underground's 85 eight-car trains. Seating capacity on a four-car train is 136.

The interior of the Waterloo & City Line's 1992 Tube Stock cars differs in having line-themed teal-coloured grab poles and handrails, and by the retention of seat armrests. The latter have long-since been removed from main 1992 Tube Stock fleet due to vandalism.

Timetabled 'ghost' running started on 12 July 1993 and passengers were carried on the modernised line from Monday 19 July 1993. The following year, on 1 April 1994, the Waterloo & City Line was transferred to London Underground.

The Waterloo & City Line trains underwent a mid-life overhaul and repainting into corporate LU livery in 2006 as part of a refurbishment programme, which caused the line to close from 1 April to 11 September. During this they retained seat armrests, long since removed from the main Central Line fleet due to vandalism, and had grab poles and other fittings repainted in the line's teal identity colour. They were also fitted with a green/blue version of the then current Central Line

seat moquette pattern. The trains are not fitted with Automatic Train Control and continue to be driven manually utilising conventional tripcock/trainstop and deadman's handle provisions.

The Central Line units were 'refreshed' between 2011 and 2012, partly in preparation for the London Olympics, the most obvious features being the introduction of the 'Barman' seating moquette pattern and strengthened external window surrounds. Another subtle change in appearance is the reduction in the amount of grey applied to cab fronts. The current fleet strength is 85 x eight-car trains on the Central Line and 5 x four-car trains on the Waterloo & City Line.

A four-car Waterloo & City Line 1992 Tube Stock train leaves Bank on its one-stop journey to Waterloo. Of note is the fixed destination label that has replaced the unreliable LCD display. The trains on this line retain a larger area of grey on the cab fronts compared to those operating on the Central.

The 1992 Tube Stock is now at the halfway point in its projected 40-year nominal lifespan. The trains perform worse than any others in the LU fleet and score the lowest in customer surveys. Much of the trains' technology is now obsolete and difficult to maintain. A Central Line Improvement Programme (CLIP) has been established by LU to ensure the trains remain safe and fit for purpose before being replaced in the Deep Tube Upgrade Programme from 2029 to 2032. Work will include a new AC propulsion system, replacing the present DC traction motors; and a new on-board computer system to supersede the outdated Data Transmission System. Other work will address corrosion damage to floors and door pillars. The stock will be made compliant to RVAR standards, including wheelchair access, LED lighting, in-car CCTV (already fitted on the W&C) and a visual passenger information system. Work is scheduled for completion by December 2022.

1995 TUBE STOCK (Northern Line)

Ordered from GEC Alsthom Metro-Cammell Ltd (now Alstom) in Birmingham, the 1995 Tube Stock was designed to replace the Northern Line's crew-operated 1956/59/62/72 Tube Stock. Trains are made up of two three-car units formed as DM-T-UNDM+UNDM-T-DM to provide a six-car consist. Body construction is from welded aluminium extrusions and includes sections from sub-assemblies made in Spain, France and Canada. The standard LU door layout is provided, with two double and one single door per side on DM cars, and two double and two single doors per side on T and UNDM cars.

Seating is all-longitudinal with 34 or 32 (DMs only) seats per car (plus 8 tip-ups) making a total of 248 on a six-car train. Moquette was originally of a line-themed black/blue/grey pattern with black armrests, though later replaced by the common Tube Lines design as fitted to the 1973 Tube Stock. Unlike on the 1996 Tube Stock, the Northern Line trains also incorporated four pairs of tip-up seats by the door stand-backs in the centre section of the saloon. Six LED scrolling visual display units operate under automatic control in each car, along with automated audio DVA station announcements and a driver-operable Public Address system. In the cab all controls, indications and platform CCTV monitors are situated directly in the train operator's line of sight. The passenger emergency alarm equipment offers two-way speech with the driver. Other safety and security-related provision includes in-car CCTV video recording equipment, whilst on the outside there are rubber inter-car gap protectors at the car ends to prevent passengers falling or being pushed in the space between cars (later retro-fitted to most other LU trains).

1995 Tube Stock 'D'-end DM car 51723 heads up a southbound train entering Woodside Park. This section of the Underground was taken over from the LNER in 1940 as part of the 1935-1940 New Works Programme.

A 'refreshed' Trailer car at Waterloo showing the blanked-off PDC buttons on the door leaves and blue seating, grab poles and handrails now fitted internally.

DM cars are fitted with mechanical couplers and Automatic Wedgelock couplers are only provided on UNDMs to facilitate coupling within a six-car train. The trains are equipped with fully-blended dynamic regenerative/rheostatic and EP friction tread brakes with load control and slip/slide protection. The AC traction motor control equipment uses Insulated Gate Bipolar Transistor (IGBT) technology instead of the gate-turn-off thyristors used on the 1996 Tube Stock. De-icing equipment is fitted to 26 trailer.

The first train was delivered in December 1996, with further trains arriving over extended periods. Entry into passenger service began on 12 June 1998 and they gradually started to replace the older types of stock. The trains were fully-equipped for OPO as delivered and worked in this mode from the outset. The fleet replacement was completed on 27 January 2000, when the final train of 1959 Tube Stock ran on the Northern Line. This was the last occasion that guards were used on regular LU passenger services, though drivers can still perform this role on certain heritage operations. By this time, 97 out of the 106 new trains had been commissioned for service, which was sufficient to provide the then 84-train peak-hour service. The other nine trains then gradually entered passenger service, the last being on 10 April 2001.

Train protection was originally by conventional tripcock/trainstop and dead-man's handle, however from 2013 ATO/ATP was progressively introduced on the Northern Line under a new Transmission Based Train Control (TBTC) signalling system. The conversion took place in stages, with train switching modes at pre-determined 'migration points'. The first section of TBTC went live between High Barnet and West Finchley on 17 February 2013 and the last, from Chalk Farm to Edgware, was completed on 1 June 2014. The trains themselves were modified for ATO/ATP operation in Edgware stabling sheds.

Between 2013 and 2015 all cars were given a mid-life 'refresh' in Morden depot. This included the yellow saloon grab poles and handrails being replaced by blue, new flooring in contrasting colours, blue 'Barman' seat moquette (though the black armrests were retained) and an external repaint. Another change was the blanking off or removal of the disused PDC buttons and installation of illuminated internal 'doors closing' visuals. To comply with RVAR rules dedicated wheelchair spaces were provided in trailer cars. The first train so treated re-entered service in May 2013 and all 106 were completed by April 2015. An extension to Battersea Power Station via Nine Elms is under construction and to cater for this, plus increases in services overall, an order for 27 additional trains is to be placed. This will consist of 172 cars and provide 17 six car trains for the Northern Line, plus 10 seven car trains for the Jubilee Line. The new trains are expected to resemble the existing 1995/96 Tube Stock fleet in appearance and layout but with modern operating systems. The Jubilee Line trains will be delivered first as they have the stronger business case, with the Northern Line batch following on afterwards.

Two dedicated wheelchair spaces are now provided in each 1995 Tube stock trailer car, with the areas made more prominent by the fitting of two transverse partitions in the centre of the car. Flooring is colour-contrasted and the internal colour relief is now predominantly blue.

1996 TUBE STOCK (Jubilee Line)

The 1996 Tube Stock is similar in appearance to the 1995 Tube Stock and both fleets were designed concurrently by GEC Alsthom Metro-Cammell. Trains were initially formed in 6-cars as DM-T-UNDM+UNDM+T-DM, with body layout, doors, coupling, braking and seating generally matching those of the Northern Line trains. The tip-up seats were omitted however and replaced by 'perches', resulting in a reduction in capacity from 248 to 200. Interior panels were mostly off-white, with yellow grab poles and handrails, and areas of turquoise at car ends around doorways and at ceiling level. Seat moquette was of a mauve/black/white/turquoise pattern, replaced from 2005 by the Tube Lines design. As per the 1995 Tube Stock, construction took place in Birmingham, though included sub-assembled parts manufactured in Canada and mainland Europe, and the initial build occurred between 1995 and 1998. A total of 20 trailer cars carry de-icing equipment.

Additional trains had been required following the authorisation in 1990 of the Jubilee Line Extension (JLE) from Green Park to Stratford. As the line's existing 1983 Tube Stock was comparatively new, an early proposal was to retain the latter in rebuilt form and operate a mixed fleet of old and new trains. In order to give a common appearance, the 1996 Tube Stock (and 1995 Stock) adopted the body profile of the 1983 Stock, including small side windows, instead of perhaps following on from the 1992 Tube Stock design. The new trains entered service on the existing Stanmore – Charing Cross section of the Jubilee progressively from Christmas Eve 1997 and began replacing the 1983 Tube Stock on a one-for-one basis until only the new stock was running by July 1998.

Initially trains ran under colour light

The Jubilee Line's 1996 Tube Stock closely resembles the 1995 Tube Stock and were built concurrently. As on a number of LU rolling stock types, higher-intensity headlights have been fitted in recent years.

signals with standard tripcock/trainstop and deadman's handle protection. Although conversion to ATO/ATP was always planned, there were doubts about the reliability of the Westinghouse 'distance-to-go' signalling system originally chosen. Late in the day a decision was made to instal traditional colour light signals and trainstops on the JLE instead. The first new section of line, from Stratford to North Greenwich, opened on 14 May 1999. This was extended as far as Waterloo on 24 September 1999, and the two halves of the Jubilee were finally joined between Waterloo and Green Park on 20 November 1999. Subsequently, the Seltrac S40 'moving block' system was chosen and installation work commenced. Stage 1 of the new signalling was commissioned on 29 December 2010 between Dollis Hill and Charing Cross/Stratford. Stage 2, between Stanmore and Dollis Hill, went live on 26 June 2011 and completed the project. The trains themselves were fitted out for ATO/ATP in Stratford Market depot.

From the start provision had been made for adding a seventh car to each train. A further batch of cars was subsequently built by Alstom between 2005 and 2006. As well as lengthening the existing stock to seven-cars, four extra complete trains were also supplied, bringing the line total to 63 trains. The additional trailer cars were inserted into the existing 'D' units over the 2005-06 Christmas period, when the entire line was closed, and increased seat capacity to 232 per train. The new cars were initially easily identifiable as they were fitted with the original design of seat material. The new train formation became DM–T–UNDM+UNDM–ST–T–DM ('ST' denoting the additional 'Special Trailer').

The difference in the Sub-Surface and Tube profiles can be seen here as a southbound Metropolitan Line S Stock and northbound Jubilee Line 1996 Tube Stock pass at Willesden Green.

'Refreshed' 1996 Tube Stock cars are gaining grey grab poles, handrails and window pans, plus a contrasting floor colour in the doorway areas and thus differ in a number of ways from the treatment given to the Northern Line trains.

A mid-life 'refresh' commenced in late-2016 with the work being carried out in Stratford Market depot. The project includes the refurbishment of saloon and cab interiors, saloon glass replacement, new flooring with a colour-contrasting finish and exterior cosmetic livery enhancement. To achieve RVAR compliance, dedicated wheelchair spaces are being provided in some trailer cars and will include palm-operated passenger emergency alarms. The first 'refreshed' train re-entered service on 24 February 2017. Among the visible differences are the new floor coverings, yellow grab poles and handrails replaced by grey, window pans and ventilators changed from off-white to grey and the turquoise décor removed. As on the 1995 Tube Stock, the exterior PDC buttons have been blanked off, but those inside cars remain though still out of use. As Barman moquette is already fitted to Jubilee Line trains, the seat pattern will not change, but armrests are now blue instead of purple to match the new design. Another small cosmetic change is the removal of the now superfluous headstock stickers indicating 'TBTC' or '7 car' status. As mentioned previously, 10 extra trains are to be built to allow for Jubilee Line service upgrades and will form part of a joint order with the Northern Line.

A 2009 Tube Stock departs Brixton on a northbound service to Walthamstow Central.

2009 TUBE STOCK (Victoria Line)

The newest trains operated on the deep-level sections of LU are the Victoria Line's 2009 Tube Stock. Built by Bombardier Transportation UK, they were designed to replace the 1967 Tube Stock that had operated on the line since its opening in 1968. Construction took place at Derby between 2006 and 2011. The order for 47 trains (376 cars) was part of the Victoria Line Upgrade which also included replacing the line's original ATO signalling with a new Westinghouse DTG-R ('distance-to-go-radio') ATO/ATP system.

Bodies are manufactured from welded and huckbolted aluminium extrusions and trains are of eight cars formed DM('A')-T('B')-NDM('C')-UNDM('D')+ UNDM('D1')-NDM('C')-T('B')-DM('A1')

– the alpha-numeric codes in brackets being the official LU designations. Dimensionally the new trains are larger than those they replaced. In overall length (133m) the trains are 3m longer than the 1967 Tube Stock, making them the longest in use on LU's deep Tube lines. They are also slightly (40mm) wider than their predecessors, reflecting the Victoria Line's larger loading gauge. This extra width combined with the trains' thinner body-shell provides slightly more space for passengers, but on the other hand the larger size prevents the stock from using the connection with the Piccadilly Line at Finsbury Park and thus all deliveries to Northumberland Park depot had to be made by road.

Automatic Wedgelock couplers are

fitted to 'A' and 'A1' cars only, with the centre 'D' and 'D1' cars joined using a swing bolt coupling. Two double and one single door per side are provided on 'A' cars, and two double and two single doors per side on 'B', 'C' and 'D' cars. All doors are externally-hung and are electrically-operated instead of pneumatic for the first time on a production LU rolling stock. The doors are fitted with 'sensitive edge' safety equipment designed to stop a moving train if an object is detected as being trapped in them, even if the 'doors closed' visual has been obtained. Uniquely on LU, the train operator's position is situated on the right-hand side of the cab, reflecting the fact that most Victoria Line platforms are on what is traditionally regarded as the 'offside'. As the line runs entirely in tunnels, with only Northumberland Park depot above ground, no de-icing provision is present.

The trains are the first on LU to comply with the RVAR as-built and include door threshold lighting, colour-contrasting fittings, plus dedicated wheelchair spaces in the UNDM cars (with platform 'humps' installed to allow level access). Wider doors allow faster boarding and alighting of passengers, reducing dwell times in stations; whilst offset-centre grab poles assist wheelchair access. Other passenger benefits include audio announcements and electronic displays showing real-time service information, and CCTV in every car for improved security.

Seating is a mixture of fixed and tip-up and all in longitudinal form. There are 32 fixed seats plus 4 tip-ups each in 'A', 'B', and 'C' cars. 'D' cars have 30 fixed seats plus 6 tip-ups but the latter must be vacated if the area is required for a wheelchair. This means a complete train has 252 fixed seats plus 36 tip-ups making a total of 288. Interior décor is mainly white with contrasting line-themed light blue grab poles and handrails. Seat moquette is 2-tone blue with red and white relief. External livery is LU corporate.

Braking is controlled by the Knorr-Bremse EP2002 system, which employs data bus links along the train to improve effectiveness, and the trains are capable of regenerative braking at 790V, significantly improving their energy efficiency.

The first train entered passenger service on 21 July 2009 and successive deliveries allowed the 1967 Tube Stock to gradually be withdrawn, with the last operating on 30 June 2011.

Opposite Another internal view of a 2009 Tube Stock. After nearly a decade in service interiors are now showing some signs of wear with seat moquette and flooring becoming discoloured.

Right The proposed design for the front of a Piccadilly Line New Tube for London (NTfL) train.

Below A possible NTfL interior view showing walk-through cars made possible by articulation. The aim is to create a modern ambience yet also draw inspiration from the design heritage of TfL and LT.

New Tube for London

A fleet of 250 new tube trains is scheduled for delivery from 2023 to be introduced, in conjunction with new signalling, on the Piccadilly, Bakerloo, Central and Waterloo & City lines. In common with the latest sub-surface trains, the cars will be walk-through. The new trains and signalling are together expected to increase capacity on the Piccadilly by 60% and give a 25% increase on the Bakerloo and Central lines.

UNDERGROUND SURFACE STOCK TRAINS

S7 AND S8 STOCK
(Circle, District, Hammersmith & City and Metropolitan Lines)

The S Stock is now the standard and only type of train in use on LU's sub-surface lines, having replaced the previous A, C and D Stock fleets. Although the D Stock was deemed capable of another ten years' reliable usage, it was felt there were more advantages of having a single design operating on the Circle, District, Hammersmith & City and Metropolitan Lines, and one ready to be easily adapted for ATO. It also enabled the elimination of 100% single-leaf passenger door stock.

The S Stock exists in two variants: the S7 is a seven-car version for the Circle, District and Hammersmith & City and District Lines, whilst the S8 is formed of eight-cars and works only on the Metropolitan Line. The trains were built by Bombardier Transport UK at Derby between 2008 and 2014. The combined S7 and S8 fleet comprises 192 trains (1402 cars +2) of standardised design, one of the largest orders ever placed in the UK. The trains embody several innovations. They are the first London Underground trains with air-conditioning, which is spread over two systems so that 50% capacity remains if one system fails. They are also the first LU trains to be designed in a 'walk through' format with wide gang-ways and cars connected by internal and external bellows and sliding floor plates. The inside of the train is thus one contin-uous saloon, providing improved capacity, security and passenger flow.

An eastbound Hammersmith & City Line S7 Stock train arriving at Barking. The train will reverse via the sidings as opposed to using the bay road platform on the left. The S7 fleet forms a common pool for the Circle, District and Hammersmith & City Lines.

As with the 2009 Tube Stock from the same manufacturer, car bodies are of welded and huckbolted aluminium extrusion construction. All cars have three sets of externally-hung double doors per side, those nearest the driving cabs being slightly narrower in width. Doors are electrically-operated but are screw-driven instead of using conventional door arms, and are provided with obstacle detection and sensitive edge equipment to prevent 'dragging' incidents. At stations doors are opened by the driver, but close after around 45 seconds to conserve heat in winter and assist the air-conditioning system in summer. PDC buttons are provided though, allowing individual doors to be reopened by passengers. Selective Door Opening (SDO) is present at a number of stations where the platforms are too short to accommodate the full length of a train. SDO is particularly prevalent on the Notting Hill Gate – Baker Street section of the Circle Line, where seven-car S7s replaced the much shorter six-car C Stock.

Each train is regarded as being a single unit and is fully-reversible and all are finished in LU corporate livery. S7 Stock is formed DM-M1-MS-MS-M2-M1-DM (or reverse) whilst S8 Stock is DM-M1-M2-MS-MS-M2-M1-DM. The M1, M2 and MS cars are all NDMs. Type M1 is a conventional NDM and included in all train formations. M2 cars are not essential components. Originally it was intended that the C Stock would be replaced by trains containing no M2 cars but it was subsequently decided that all trains would have at least one M2 car, with eight-car trains including two. The middle cars are

Motor Shoe (MS) cars which can be uncoupled to split trains in depots for maintenance. NDM cars with de-icing equipment are given the sub-code M2D and there are 42 S7 and 27 S8 cars so fitted. Every axle on a train is motored, maximising acceleration rates and also improving braking capability.

Traction is provided by AC asynchronous electric motors driven using IGBT controllers and DC 630V supply and the train is capable of regenerative braking at 790V. Power upgrades are progressively increasing the line voltage to 750V allowing regenerative braking at 890V, improving the energy efficiency of trains.

Both variants share common design characteristics and specifications but they diverge in particular details that reflect the differing characters of the lines that they serve. The Circle Line, for instance, is characterised by dense, short-distance journeys which are best handled by trains with longitudinal seats and more standing room. On the other hand, passengers on the Metropolitan Line expect a higher proportion of seats on their longer commute (and of the forward/rear-facing design too) so the S8 Stock has some transverse seating provided (the A Stock it replaced had 100% transverse seating).

The District Line shares elements of both ridership characteristics and there were early plans for a compromise seating plan combining both formats. In the event though all S7 Stock have a 100% longitudinal seat layout fully-interchangeable between the District and Circle & Hammersmith Lines. Seating per car-type is as follows: DM 34 fixed seats (plus 6 tip-ups), M1/M2 32 fixed seats (plus 6 tip-ups) and MS 30 fixed seats (plus 7 tip-ups). Overall seat capacity for the S7 is 206 (plus 50 tip-ups) making 256 in all, and on the S8 262 (plus 44 tip-ups) giving a total of 306.

Interiors are finished in off-white with yellow handrails and grab poles. The seat moquette pattern combines small rectangles of green and yellow, or pink and mauve, on a black base; and represents the four lines the stock serves. Digitally-recorded CCTV allows the driver to view car interiors whilst the train is stationary. Station-based cameras transmit images by microwave to the cab so that a train's arrival, departure and platform duties can be monitored safely. An early modification saw loop 'straphangers' fitted to the horizontal handrails in cars after these were found to be sited too high for some passengers.

Passenger information is improved too. Pre-recorded DVA is brought to the Metropolitan Line for the first time (it was already present on all other lines) and two double-sided scrolling LED displays are installed in each car. The latter show the destination and the line but can also display other messages such as safety announcements. There are also two external LED displays per car and on the longer distance trains these alternate between destination, stopping pattern and line name, e.g. 'Amersham', 'All Stations', and 'Metropolitan line'.

Wedgelock couplers with pneumatic connections only are fitted to the fronts of DM cars with other cars being connected by bolted bar coupler flanges. The trains use the same Knorr-Bremse EP2002 braking system as the 2009 Tube Stock, which includes regenerative and rheostatic braking.

The inter-car 'bellows' connections of the S Stock which allow walk-though interiors are clearly apparent in this view of an eastbound District Line train at Stamford Brook.

The S7 Stock interior with all-longitudinal seating and tip-seats, plus transverse partitions defining the areas designated for priority use by wheelchair-users.

A limited number of transverse seats are fitted to the S8 Stock and reflect the often longer commuter journeys of the Metropolitan Line. Seat moquette pattern features the colours of the four lines served by S Stock.

The areas below the S8 Stock's transverse seats are easily accessible for cleaning and security.

The first line to receive S Stock was the Metropolitan from August 2010, enabling the A Stock to be replaced by September 2012. Roll-out followed on the Hammersmith & City and Circle Lines from July 2012, allowing C Stock withdrawal in June 2014. District Line S Stock operation commenced in September 2013 with the last D Stock running on 21 April 2017.

The S Stock was introduced using the standard tripcock/trainstop train protection system, with conventional manual driving and doors operated by the driver from the leading cab, but conversion to ATO was always planned. However the original proposal to use Bombardier's own CityFlow 650 signalling was abandoned in early 2014 and later replaced by a Thales Communications Based Train Control (CBTC) system similar to that used on the Jubilee and Northern lines. One consequence of this was the SSR (Sub Surface Railway) Re-signalling Project being renamed the Four Lines Modernisation Project (or 4LM). The new system will provide for full ATO/ATC with automatic door opening at stations, and will allow more intensive services to be run,

bringing about a 33% increase in capacity across all four lines by 2023.

Trains are being progressively returned to Derby for ATC fit-out by Bombardier with the first re-entering service in March 2017. Such trains can be identified by the two grey antennas fitted at roof level above the cab windscreens, and the initial section of the new CBTC is scheduled to go live in 2018.

Three trains of S7 layout were temporarily formed into eight-car formation for use on the Metropolitan Line. One reverted to S7 formation with its rightful (seventh) car but the other two remain in S7+1 formation. Both are being used as extra trains during the ATC fitment programme and one will be retained as an extra train for the Metropolitan Line extension from Croxley to Watford Junction, should this go ahead. To that end, two new cars were built and inserted into the units that originally donated a car to make up the S7+1 trains. Fleet allocation is ultimately expected to be 59 x S8 on the Metropolitan Line, 80 x S7 on the District Line, and 53 x S7 on the Circle & Hammersmith & City Lines, with the S7s being completely interchangeable.

Opposite An eastbound District Line S7 Stock at Aldgate East.

Opposite A Metropolitan Line S8 Aldgate-bound arrives at Baker Street platform 3, showing the platform lengthening carried out here for the new trains.

HERITAGE TRAINS

From time-to-time heritage trains operate over parts of the network. All such rolling stock must hold a Certificate of Technical Conformance (CTC) to run on LU infrastructure and are either owned by the LT Museum or hired in for the occasion. The LT Museum has a 4-car 1938 Tube Stock unit, Met Rly electric loco No.12 'Sarah Siddons', 'Jubilee Coach' 353 and Milk Van No.4 (as a support vehicle).

An ex-BR '4-TC' unit is normally used to carry passengers. Privately-owned stock used in recent years includes Met Rly 'E' class loco No.1, GWR 'Prairie Tank' 5521 (as 'L150' in LT maroon), the Bluebell Railway's Ashbury coaches and Class 20 loco 20142 (in Met Railway/LT maroon). Privately-owned 1960 Tube Stock 3906-4927-3907 has also held a CTC and been used to operate tours on London Underground.

The London Transport Museum's four-car 1938 Tube Stock at South Ealing whilst operating an enthusiasts' railtour on the District and Piccadilly lines.

Cravens Heritage Trains' three-car 1960 Tube Stock seen at North Weald station on the Epping – Ongar Railway during an LT-themed weekend. Motive power was provided by two Schöma diesel locos from the TransPlant fleet and which are coupled at the rear.

Privately-owned Class 20 diesel locomotive 20142 is certificated for use on LU and carries a joint LT/Metropolitan Railway maroon livery.

Ex-Metropolitan Railway 'E'-Class No.1 approaches Earl's Court in 2013 as part of the LU150 celebrations. Also visible is Milk Van 4, 'Jubilee Coach' 353 and part of an Ashbury coach.

Ex-Metropolitan Railway electric loco 'Sarah Siddons' hauls the Bluebell Railway's Ashbury coaches rake through High Street Kensington on a LU150 working from Moorgate to Lillie Bridge depot via Olympia.

Ex-GWR Prairie Tank 5521 is also used on LU heritage trains and has been given pseudo-LT steam locomotive livery as 'L 150'.

HERITAGE TRAINS

LT MUSEUM-OWNED
1938 Tube Stock.

DM(A)	T	NDM	DM(D)
10012	012256	12048	11012

Ex-Met Rly electric locomotive 'Sarah Siddons'.

12

Ex-BR '4-TC' unit.

DTSO	TFK	TBSK	DTSO
76297	71163	70823	76324

Ex-BR Mk1 Carriage.

BSK
35011

Ex-Met Rly 'Jubilee Coach'.

353

Ex-Met Rly Milk Van (support vehicle).

4

Ex-LMS Engineers Inspection Saloon (undergoing restoration at Eastleigh Works).

45029

PRIVATELY-OWNED
Ex-Met Rly Ashbury Coaches.

368	387	394	412

1960 Tube Stock.

DM(A)	T	DM(D)
3906	4927	3907

Ex-Met Rly 'E' Class steam locomotive.

1

Ex-GWR 'Prairie Tank' steam locomotive.

5521 (L150)

Ex-BR Class 20 diesel locomotives.

20142	20189 (L189)	20227

LONDON OVERGROUND

Arriva Rail London is the Train Operating Company (TOC) responsible for running the London Overground network, which it does under a Concession Agreement with Transport for London (TfL), having taken over from former concessionaire London Overground Rail Operations Ltd (LOROL) on 13 November 2016. Its routes comprise the North London Line (Stratford to Richmond), the West London Line (Willesden Junction to Clapham Junction), the extended East London Line (Highbury & Islington to West Croydon/ Crystal Palace/Clapham Junction), the Euston to Watford DC Line, the Gospel Oak to Barking line, the Lea Valley Lines (Liverpool Street to Enfield, Chingford and Cheshunt), and the isolated Romford to Upminster branch. The East London Line, between Whitechapel and New Cross and New Cross Gate was part of London Underground until December 2007. Most other lines were taken over from the Silverlink Metro in November 2007, the exceptions being the Lea Valley and Romford to Upminster services which were acquired from Abellio Greater Anglia on 31 May 2015.

When London Overground took over the Silverlink Metro services it inherited a number of Class 313 AC/DC dual-system EMUs (and a small number of DC-only Class 508s) as well as the Class 150 DMUs used on the Gospel Oak to Barking line. These trains presented an outdated image and were not capable of economic improvement, so the existing livery was retained, minus the Silverlink branding, and TfL ordered a fleet of new trains designed specifically to meet the needs of London Overground's 'metro' style operations.

A Class 378/2 *Capitalstar* calls at South Acton on a section of the North London Line equipped with 3rd rail only.

The Class 378/2s are fitted for both 3rd rail and overhead current collection. The latter mode is in use here at Camden Road on this Richmond to Stratford North London Line train. Like all Class 378 trains this unit is now formed of five cars.

CLASS 378 UNITS (East London Line, North London Line, South London Line, West London Line, and Watford DC Line)

The introduction of new trains was a central part of TfL's vision of rejuvenating and combining various run-down inner suburban railway lines under the London Overground brand. The Class 378 was developed as part of Bombardier's *Electrostar* family of EMUs but has been given the title *Capitalstar* by TfL. The trains were built at Derby and featured bodies with welded aluminium underframes, sides and roof combined with steel ends. Each car has two sets of PDC-equipped double doors per side. They are of the internal-sliding type as these are quicker in operation than the 'plug' doors used on most modern commuter trains. Internally, seating is low-density and wholly-longitudinal.

In their present-day 5-car formation, each Class 378 seats 146 passengers. Individual seat provision is DMSO (36 Standard), MSO (40 Standard), and PTSO and TSO (34 Standard, 6 tip-ups, plus two wheelchair spaces). All seating is transverse and gangway connections are 'walk-through' to aid passenger movement. The units introduced the new LO livery, which was clearly influenced by the modern LU scheme but using orange instead of red as the door colour. Orange had been chosen as the 'signature' colour of LO and this was reflected in the grab poles and other internal fittings also. These were also the first trains to be fitted with the bespoke LO orange and brown seat moquette pattern (with a lighter version indicating priority seats).

Other innovations include air-conditioning and passenger information system screens both internally and externally. Cameras mounted on the body sides transmit images to the cab as opposed to the platform-mounted equipment used on LU trains. To start with, some trains operated in crew mode with a guard on the NLL but DOO is now standard across the whole of LO. Couplers are Dellner 12 and brakes a combination of disc and regenerative. In addition to Automatic Warning System (AWS) and Driver's Safety Device (DSD), tripcocks are fitted for use on the Queen's Park – Harrow & Wealdstone section of the Bakerloo Line shared with LU trains. De-icing arrangements are required on the 3rd rail sections and five Class 378/1 and five Class 378/2 units are fitted with this equipment.

Initial operation commenced on the North London Line from 29 July 2009. Trains were then in 3-car form and dual-fitted so as to run on both the 3rd rail and 25kV overhead line sections of the route. They were to eventually number 24 and were classed as 378/0. The new trains allowed the gradual withdrawal of the Class 313 and 508 units previously used by Silverlink Metro on the North London, West London and Watford DC Lines. In addition, twenty 4-car trains were ordered for the extended East London Line (ELL). These were to be DC-only for 3rd rail use and designated as Class 378/1. Apart from the lack of pantograph and extra carriage, appearance was virtually identical to the existing Class 378/0 fleet.

The East London Line reopened on 27 April 2009 between Dalston Junction and New Cross/New Cross Gate, and was extended to Crystal Palace and West Croydon from 23 May 2010 with all services worked by Class 378/1s.

In 2007 TfL had placed an additional order for 24 extra carriages to extend the Class 378/0 units to four cars and on completion of this the trains were reclassi-fied as Class 378/2. In addition three extra four-car Class 378/1s were ordered for the ELL. A further seven four-car units were ordered in 2008 and another three in 2009, bringing the total number of *Capitalstars* to 57. In February 2013, 57 more carriages were ordered to allow all Class 378s to be lengthened to five cars and this was accomplished by January 2016. Train formation is now as follows: Class 378/1 DMSO-MSO-TSO-MSO-DMSO and Class 378/2 DMSO-MSO-PTSO-MSO-DMSO.

The current fleet deployment comprises 20 Class 378/1 units that are DC-only and operate on the East London Line and the South London Line. As such they replaced Southern's Class 456 EMUs and, indi-rectly, LU's A Stock. In addition 37 Class 378/2 units are AC/DC dual-fitted and operate on the North London Line, West London Line and Watford DC Line. These replaced the Class 313 and 508 EMUs. The 378/2s can run on the East London Line and South London Line if required but the lack of a pantograph means the Class 378/1s are route-bound. The trains are owned by ROSCO QW Rail Leasing.

Class 378 interiors are designed for high-capacity passenger loadings and feature walk-through carriages and all-longitudinal seating. Note also the colour-contrast flooring, door 'threshold' lighting and extensive use of the orange LO brand colour.

LO's only passenger-carrying diesel trains are the Class 172/0 *Turbostars* used on the Gospel Oak – Barking Line. Unit 172008 is about to shunt east-to-west at South Tottenham during the period services were suspended east of the station for overhead electrification work.

CLASS 172/0 UNITS (Gospel Oak – Barking Line)

London Overground operates eight two-car Class 172 diesel multiple units (DMUs) on the Gospel Oak to Barking Line, replacing the Class 150 units inherited from Silverlink Metro. Diesel trains were required on this route as it was not electrified at the time LO took over the service as a cost/benefit case for this had not yet been identified.

The trains were built by Bombardier at Derby as a variant of their *Turbostar* family of DMUs and entered service in 2010. Body construction combines welded aluminium and bolt-on steel ends and formation is DMS-DMS. Two sets of passenger doors per side are provided on each car of the double-leaf sliding plug type and PDC is in use.

Seating is of the 2+2 transverse high-back facing/unidirectional style with 64 seats in the 594xxx DMS, and 60 + 2 wheelchair spaces in the adjoining 593xxx

vehicle. This is fewer than on the Class 150 DMUs they replaced, but increased room is provided for standing passengers, together with wider aisles at the doorways which helps reduce dwell time at stations. Opening windows are not provided as the trains are fitted with air-conditioning. Public address, CCTV and a passenger information system are provided. Standard LO décor is applied both internally and externally. BSI couplers are fitted and braking is Air EP. Train protection is through conventional main line DSD, AWS and Train Protection and Warning System (TPWS). Ownership lies with ROSCO Angel Trains.

Funding for 25kV AC overhead electrification was finally provided in June 2013 and the work carried out between 2016 and 2017, with the expectation that the Class 172s would be replaced by 4-car Class 710 Bombardier *Aventra* units in 2018.

CLASS 315 UNITS (Lea Valley Lines and Romford to Upminster Line)

Seventeen Class 315 units are operated on routes out of Liverpool Street as a result of the takeover of Lea Valley Line services from Abellio Greater Anglia in May 2015. The trains were originally built by BREL York in 1980-81 for BR Great Eastern suburban routes and replaced the LNER-derived Class 306 units. The overall design was derived from the experimental Class 445 '4PEP' and 446 '2PEP' units introduced on the BR Southern Region in 1971-72. These introduced such innovations as air-operated sliding doors, open saloons and low-backed seating. Although some of these ideas had featured in designs inherited from the LMS and LNER, and on the Glasgow area Class 303 'Blue Trains', they were nevertheless generally in complete contrast to BR's traditional design of suburban commuter train using slam-doors, compartments and/or semi-open interiors.

The Class 315s are formed into four-car units as DMSO-TSO-PTSO-DMSO, are standard class only and can operate in multiple. Construction combines an aluminium alloy body and a steel frame. Each carriage has two sets of double doors per side, all internal-sliding, and PDC is in use. Seating capacity is 318 in a low-back 2+2 or 2+3 high-density layout. Specific seat provision is DMSO (74 plus 2 tip-ups), TSO (86 plus 4 tip-ups) and PTSO (84 plus 8 tip-ups and 2 wheelchair spaces).

Unlike the similar-looking and now replaced Class 313 rolling stock inherited by LO from Silverlink Metro, the trains are equipped for overhead electrification only. Tightlock couplers are fitted, braking is Westcode and rheostatic, and train protection ensured through DSD and AWS.

Since May 2015 the former Abellio Greater Anglia Class 315 fleet has been split between LO and TfL Rail. Unit 315801 in full LO livery stands at Seven Sisters forming a Lea Valley Lines working to Liverpool Street. These trains can operate from overhead electrification only.

Interior refurbishment of the Class 315s was carried out between 2015 and 2016 by Bombardier Ilford. Grab poles and seating were changed to LO standard orange and other areas deep-cleaned, but the luggage rack handrails have remained in Abellio red.

As delivered, livery was BR blue and grey, later replaced by NSE red, white and blue; and various schemes have been carried during the privatisation era. By the time transfer to LO took place trains were in Abellio Greater Anglia plain white livery with red doors, and initial operations saw them retain this in de-branded form but with the addition of LO roundels on car sides.

The trains were refurbished for TOC 'one' Railway at Bombardier Derby between 2004 and 2008, during which they were fitted with 'easy to clean' vinyl flooring and new window frames. Further work was undertaken in 2013 when in use by Abellio Greater Anglia. The work was carried out at Bombardier Ilford and included ceiling-mounted LED passenger information displays, wheelchair bays, priority seating and communicating door handles and luggage rack handrails changed to Abellio corporate red. A third refurbishment was carried out at Bombardier Ilford from 2015 to 2016 on behalf of LO. Internally, units gained orange grab poles and seat grab handles and standard LO orange and brown seating moquette, though the red luggage rack handrails remain. Externally, full LO livery has been applied. The trains are maintained at Ilford depot and are owned by ROSCO Eversholt Rail (UK). They are scheduled for replacement by Class 710 *Aventras* from mid-2018 onwards.

CLASS 317 UNITS (Lea Valley Lines and Romford to Upminster Line)

Two sub-classes of Class 317 units were inherited from Abellio Greater Anglia in May 2015. These comprise eight Class 317/7s and six Class 317/8s. All were built at BREL Derby or York between 1980-81 for use on the newly-electrified route between Moorgate/St Pancras and Bedford. Entry into service was delayed due to a dispute over DOO and the existing First Generation DMUs on the line were not replaced until 1983.

The body profile is based on the Mk3 carriage design and construction is all-steel. Door provision is two double each side per carriage, internal-sliding, and with PDC. Both classes are fitted with Tightlock couplers and Westinghouse air brakes, are equipped for overhead electrification only, and can operate in multiple. Livery during BR ownership was blue and grey as built, and then NSE red, white and blue from 1986. The original batch of trains was given the full classification of 317/1.

In 1987, as part of the cross-London Thameslink project, the 317/1s were displaced by dual-voltage Class 319s and began use on outer-suburban services from Euston. A batch of new Class 321 EMUs was introduced on this route from 1989, leading to the 317/1s transferring to West Anglia and Great Northern routes out of Liverpool Street and King's Cross respectively. Here they worked alongside a second build of 317s which had been introduced in 1985-86 and designated 317/2.

A small fleet of Class 317 units was also acquired from Abellio Greater Anglia in May 2015 as part of the Lea Valley Lines takeover. Slightly more numerous are the Class 317/7 variant which can be identified by their rounded cab roof domes. These trains were formerly used on Stansted Express duties until displaced by new Class 379s in 2011.

All of those operated by LO were originally of the 317/1 variety, before being modified for use on the Stansted Express service. The trains now identified as Class 317/7s were converted by Railcare Wolverhampton in 2000 and given luggage racks and a modified front end design which included a rounded roof dome and revised head and tail light clusters. Other changes were that lino flooring was replaced by carpets, new internal panels were fitted and a wheelchair space was provided in TSO carriages. One toilet was refurbished and the other replaced by a RVAR-compliant accessible toilet. Those seats in a 2+3 layout were removed and replaced by new high-back seating fitted as 2+2. The First Class area in the TCO (now TSO) was removed, re-sited in one of the DTSO (now DTCO) vehicles, and given high-back 2+1 seats. Some seats in each carriage were taken out and replaced by two vertical luggage racks to cater for airport traffic. In 2005-06, further units were given similar but not identical internal treatment at Wabtec Doncaster and reclassified as Class 317/8.

The 317s operated by LO come in two different formations. The 317/7s are DTSO-MSO-TSO-DTCO and seat 194 with 172 Standard Class seats and 22 de-classified First Class seats. Individual carriage capacity is DTSO (52 Standard), MSO (62 Standard), TSO (42 Standard) and DTCO (16 Standard/22 First). The 317/8s are DTSO-MSO-TCO-DTSO and seat 265 with 245 Standard Class seats and 20 de-classified First Class seats. Individual carriage capacity is DTSO (66 Standard), MSO (71 Standard) and TCO (42 Standard/20 First). Train protection is by DSD and AWS.

Both sub-classes were displaced from Stansted Express duties in 2011 by new Class 379 trains and thereafter used in general traffic. They were subsequently refurbished under Abellio Greater Anglia between 2013 and 2015. Upon acquisition by LO in 2015 all carriages gained roundels and a programme of 'refreshing' began at Bombardier Ilford. This saw the de-branded Abellio Greater Anglia or National Express liveries replaced by LO standard. Interiors gained orange grab poles and seat handles, and the high-backed seats were re-trimmed in orange and brown moquette. From July 2017 the toilet compartments, including those wheelchair-accessible, were locked out of use. The trains are maintained at Ilford depot and owned by ROSCO Angel Trains. They are also scheduled for replacement by Class 710s from 2018.

CLASS 710 UNITS (Gospel Oak – Barking Line, Lea Valley Lines, Romford to Upminster Line and Watford DC Line)

In 2014 TfL announced that longer diesel trains were to be ordered for the Gospel Oak – Barking Line as the existing Class 172s were unable to cope with the increase in demand experienced on this route. The original plan was to introduce three- or four-car trains but this idea was cancelled when the Government authorised the electrification of the line using the 25kV overhead system. A revised scheme was proposed in April 2014 and involved the supply of 39 four-car EMUs. These would be allocated as follows: 8 for Gospel Oak – Barking, 30 for the Lea Valley Lines, and one for the isolated Romford – Upminster shuttle. A further 6 trains were then ordered for the Watford DC Line, which would allow the existing Class 378s to augment services on the ELL and NLL.

July 2015 saw TfL announce that 45 trains (180 vehicles) had been ordered from Bombardier and would be of the manufacturer's *Aventra* EMU design. This is a development of the *Electrostar* family but trains will be lighter and more energy-efficient than previous designs, with all-welded bodies and two wide double doors each side per car.

Walk-through gangway connections will increase capacity and reduce station dwell times. Innovations will include USB charging points for passenger use and internal digital screen advertising. The sloping cab front features a single wide windscreen and gives a very European appearance. Exact unit formations and individual carriage numbers were provisional at time of writing, but the trains will come in two batches: The 31 Class 710/1 will be AC-only and operate on the Lea Valley Lines and the Romford shuttle. Seating will be a mix of longitudinal and transverse and similar to that on LU's S8 Stock. The remaining 14 Class 710/2 will be dual-fitted for AC and DC electrification and run on the Gospel Oak – Barking and Watford DC lines. Seating on these will be all longitudinal in the style of the S7 Stock and Class 378s. Delivery is expected to commence in 2018 and TfL have an option of a further 24 trains. The *Aventra* design has also been chosen for Crossrail (as Class 345) and these trains are described later.

CLASS 09/0 (Willesden TMD)

One Class 09/0 0-6-0 diesel shunting locomotive is retained by LO at Willesden TMD for general duties within the yard. The loco is officially numbered 09007 but carries its pre-TOPS identity of D3671 and 1960s BR green livery and logos.

Artist's impression of the new Class 710 Bombardier *Aventra* due for delivery to LO in 2018.

TfL RAIL

The majority of the Class 315s passed to TfL Rail in May 2015 and all are now in corporate white livery with blue skirt, doors and roundels as on this example at Seven Kings.

TfL Rail runs the 'Metro' stopping service on the Great Eastern Main Line between Liverpool Street and Shenfield. Operations commenced in May 2015 and took over from Abellio Greater Anglia. The transfer was a precursor to the opening of Crossrail, as the latter will also be run by TfL. It was decided that the Crossrail brand would not be applied to existing rolling stock and 'TfL Rail' identity is used with a blue skirt colour and roundel. In February 2016 it was announced that the new east-west railway (also referred to as Crossrail 1) would be formally known as the Elizabeth Line and therefore signage at stations and on the new trains will ultimately reflect this. Management is by MTR Corporation (Crossrail) Ltd on behalf of TfL.

TfL Rail's Class 315 trains were also refurbished at Bombardier Ilford, but with blue being used as the internal signature colour. Note the lighter moquette pattern variant used to denote a priority seat.

CLASS 315 UNITS
(Liverpool Street – Shenfield Line)

May 2015 saw a total of 43 four-car Class 315 units acquired from the Abellio Greater Anglia franchise. These had formed part of a common pool of Abellio 315s that were also used on the Lea Valley Lines and were now split between LO and TfL Rail. The technical specifications and formation of the TfL Rail units are identical to those operated by LO and have been described earlier.

Although TfL Rail's Class 315s were scheduled for replacement by new Class 345 trains from mid-2017, a programme of deep-cleaning and a 'refresh' was carried out at Bombardier Ilford. Internally cars were signed to TfL standards with line diagrams fitted and most lettering is now in New Johnston. Handrails and grab poles were changed to blue and the low-backed 2+2 and 2+3 seats re-trimmed in predominantly blue and grey moquette. All trains were repainted in a TfL Rail livery combining a white body with blue doors and skirt, and clearly having an affinity to the LU, LO and London Tramlink colour schemes. Initially, as with the LO Class 315s, trains ran in previous operators' liveries, though with blue 'TfL Rail' roundels applied.

These trains are also maintained at Ilford depot and owned by ROSCO Eversholt Rail (UK). Delivery of the new Class 345 trains commenced in late-2016 and the first entered service on 22nd June 2017, allowing the gradual withdrawal of the 315s to begin.

CLASS 345 UNITS (Elizabeth Line)

A total of 70 new trains have been ordered from Bombardier Derby as part of the Crossrail Project. Like the Class 710s of LO, these are also part of *Aventra* family, but will differ in being of nine-car formation and having three sets of sliding plug double doors each side per car instead of two. Coupling and braking arrangements follow that provided on the Class 710s. The trains are equipped for 25kV AC overhead electrification only but can be retro-fitted with 750V DC shoe-gear to allow for a future extension to Gravesend.

The trains will work under a number of different signalling systems. In the central core tunnel sections CBTC will be installed to allow ATO/ATP and platform edge doors will be used. On the surface, the primary form of train protection will ultimately be by the European Train Control System (ETCS) but the trains are also compatible with the earlier 'legacy' systems (i.e. AWS/TPWS) in use on the national rail network.

Seating is a mix of 450 longitudinal, transverse 2+2 facing and tip-up, and there are four wheelchair spaces in the centre TSO car. No toilets or First Class seats are provided. The trains are air-conditioned and free Wi-Fi and 4G will be available. Passenger information displays will be continuously updated. Interior décor includes dark floors plus grey window surrounds and ceilings. Grab poles, straphangers and seat armrests are black; whilst coving panels contrast in white. Seat moquette is predominately purple in colour with the pattern following TfL design conventions. With purple being the Crossrail identity colour early drawings showed an external livery of white body with purple skirt, doors and roundels, being similar to that used by LU and LO. This was later changed to a scheme of purple below windows and black above, white doors and roof, and with areas of white and lighter purple at car ends. Improvements in headlight technology mean that yellow cab fronts are no longer mandatory on Network Rail and this area is coloured black instead.

Three sliding plug-type double doors are provided on each side of TfL Rail's Class 345 cars. Livery is blue body, white doors and roof with black window surrounds. Some areas of purple are also used and can be seen on ends of the adjacent carriages.

The full nine-car formation is DMSO(A)-PMSO(A)-MSO(A)-MSO(B)*-TSO-MSO(C)*-MSO(D)-PMSO(B)-DMSO(B) but the first 15 trains will be delivered as seven-cars with the asterisked MSO cars omitted. This is because their dedicated terminal platforms at Liverpool Street (high level) are not long enough to accommodate nine-car trains. When through-running begins between Paddington (low level) and Liverpool Street (low level) in 2019 the extra carriages will be inserted and all trains will be in nine-car form. The Class 345s initially running between Heathrow Terminal 4 and Paddington (high level) will be of nine-car form from the start.

Daytime test running on the Great Eastern Main Line commenced on 15 February 2017 using unit 345002 and the first train to carry passengers entered service on 22nd June 2017 using unit 345005. TfL Rail services using nine-car Class 345s will begin in 2018 replacing the Heathrow Connect trains out of Paddington. Maintenance of the fleet will be carried out in Old Oak Common depot and TfL have an option of a further 19 trains to accommodate a future increase of frequencies and a possible extension to Gravesend. In July 2017 this was exercised with four extra nine-car units being ordered.

Opposite Advances in rail headlight technology have allowed the Class 345s to dispense with yellow cab areas which have been part of the railway scene in Britain since the early-1960s.

The Class 345 *Aventra* interior features a mix of longitudinal, tip-up and 2+2 facing transverse seating. The moquette pattern is in shades of purple, and seat armrests and the majority of grab poles and handrails are coloured black. Visual passenger information is provided by ceiling-mounted video screens.

LONDON UNDERGROUND Engineers' trains

The London Underground service stock fleet is maintained and operated by 'TransPlant', a division of Tube Lines, which is itself now wholly-owned by TfL. The organisation has its origins in the 1960s when the Miscellaneous Vehicles Division was formed to operate engineers' trains from Ealing Common, Lillie Bridge and Neasden depots. In 1980 the Engineers Trains Unit was created with bases at Ealing Common, Lillie Bridge and now Ruislip. In 1980 Ealing Common was vacated and Lillie Bridge followed suit by 2016.

The mainstay of the fleet are the 29 battery locomotives built between 1964 and 1974. These comprise 18 Metro-Cammell locomotives (L20-32 built in 1964 and L15-19 built in 1970-71). The other 11 locomotives (L44-54) were built by BREL at Doncaster in 1973-74, and these allowed some older locos to be withdrawn. Six locomotives (L62-L67) were built in 1985-86 by Metro-Cammell to a much more modern design but were non-standard and ultimately found to be unreliable. They were withdrawn after a just few years' service and finally scrapped in 2012.

Apart from L62-67, all of the battery locomotives described above had buffers which were hinged up and back when coupling to vehicles of Tube Stock height and to a design basically unchanged (apart from minor variations) from that first used in 1938. All locomotives have a cab at each end and are built to Tube loading gauge. They are able to operate either on current or from battery power and are normally used on engineers' trains, mainly at start or end of traffic and during Engineering Hours within possessions. The locos can also been seen on the network in daylight hours when proceeding to and from weekend engineering work.

Various modifications have been made to the locomotives, most noticeably the provision of high-intensity headlights, replacement of the hinged buffers by spring buffers, and the fitting of buckeye couplers. More recently, work began to modify all 29 remaining locos. This has included improved battery cell access and modernised driving cabs. The most noticeable difference is that access is now through the central 'M' doors, resulting in side cab doors being removed and additional handrails fitted to the front ends. Work on the 29th locomotive is scheduled for completion in August 2019.

For the construction and equipping of the JLE, 14 diesel locomotives were constructed by Schöma of Germany in 1995 to haul a dedicated fleet of 15 Bombardier-built general purpose wagons, four bogie well wagons and four 4-wheel cable drum wagons. The 32-tonne diesel locomotives were built to Tube loading gauge suitable for working in deep-level tunnels. They are fitted with normal-height buffers and drop-head buckeye couplers. In 1989, once construction of the JLE was complete, the locomotives and wagons were acquired by TransPlant. Ten of the locos have been converted at Ruislip depot to battery/electric operation by Clayton Equipment Ltd of Burton-upon-Trent.

Two Pilot Motor cars, former Cravens 1960 Tube Stock DM cars 3901 and 3905, continue to operate with the Track Recording Vehicle (TRV), itself converted by BREL at Derby from 1973 Tube Stock trailer 514 in 1987. The train runs on the Central, Jubilee, Northern and Piccadilly lines in an 8-week cycle. Its use on the rest of the system is generally no longer necessary following the advent of passenger rolling stock fitted with automatic track monitoring equipment. An 'Asset Inspection Train' was formed in 2010 using a four-car unit of 1972 MkI Tube Stock (and later strengthened by the inclusion of two 1967 Tube Stock DM cars in the centre). Entry into service has been protracted however and a decision was made in 2017 to extend the life of the existing TRV.

Five track maintenance tamping machines form part of the current fleet. The earliest three date from 1980 and are of Tube profile. Newer machines were bought in 2007 and 2015 but are of a size unable to pass through the smaller deep-level tunnels. In 2016 a former Tube Lines FEA-S container flat wagon, previously part of the Rail and Sleeper Delivery Train, was converted to a 'Concrete Mixing and Distribution Unit' by the addition of a demountable mixer. The mixer is powered from battery locos but also has its own diesel back-up generator. Although designed for Surface Stock lines, the hopper can be replaced by a smaller unit to allow use on the deep-level Tubes if required.

Equally important are the various cranes and wagons in the engineering fleet – including hopper wagons, general purpose wagons, well wagons, cable drum wagons, spoil/ballast wagons and rail wagons. Many of these are now considered to be outdated, time-expired and have received minimal investment, so in March 2017 an order for 66 open wagons and five flatbed wagons was placed with CRRC Shandong of China (the order reduced from 86 originally authorised in June 2016).

Another important task is the operation of Rail Adhesion Trains (RATs) in the autumn months to combat leaf-fall and is traditionally performed using former or modified passenger rolling stock. For many years the work was carried out on the Metropolitan Line by inserting converted 'Sandite' trailer 6036 within a standard four-car A Stock unit. On the Central Line, two 1962 Tube Stock trains are used, in either five-car or eight-car formation. In 2016 a new RAT was created using five cars of withdrawn D Stock, with a second train in reserve, and should allow the A Stock RAT to be retired.

The current battery locomotive fleet is also scheduled for replacement. Two prototype locos are planned, with the production vehicles subsequently obtained through a leasing arrangement. The new locomotives will be equipped with a signalling back-bone allowing compatibility with the four modern and two legacy signalling systems that will be in use on LU by 2026. They will also be designed to run on the 750V power supply upgrade implemented as part of the 4LM programme.

'DISAB 1' ballast-sucking unit comprising wagons CM955, CM951 and JLE2 in demonstration use at Ruislip depot. The units are used for removing contaminated 'wet beds', laying new ballast, drain-cleaning and collecting other miscellaneous waste.

TMM 771 is one of three Tube-profile plain line tamping machines built in 1980 by Plasser Theurer and is the only one fitted with Central Line ATP equipment. This type of tamper can operate independently or in train formation during traffic hours.

The Asset Inspection Train was converted from a former four-car unit of 1972 (Mk I) Tube Stock. Since this photo of an Uxbridge – Acton Town test working at Sudbury Town was taken, an extra two ex-1967 Tube Stock DM cars have been added in the centre of the unit to improve performance.

The Track Recording Train operates over the majority of the LU network on a periodic basis and consists of two ex-1960 Tube Stock DM cars, plus a converted ex-1973 Tube Stock trailer car. The latter forms the Track Recording Vehicle itself and measures track gauge, twist, cant, alignment, corrugation and undulation.

Most battery locomotives are now in this rebuilt form with cab side doors sealed and handrails fitted to allow safe access via the front of the loco. L 24 was built by Metro-Cammell in 1965 and was the first to be modified.

Concrete Mixing and Distribution Unit CM 932 was converted from a FEA-S container wagon by Blend Plants, Italy, in 2016. It previously formed part of Tube Lines' Rail and Sleeper Delivery Train which was built in 2006 by Marcroft & Greenbrier, Poland, but has since been disposed of. The unit enters Northfields depot between two modified battery locomotives following trials on the South Ealing test track.

TMM 774 is a plain line and points & crossings tamping machine from Franz Plasser dating from in 2007. This tamper is restricted to use on surface and sub-surface areas only.

Schöma locomotive 4 is one of fourteen delivered in 1996 for use on the construction of the Jubilee Line Extension and subsequently absorbed into the TransPlant fleet. It is now one of ten locos converted from diesel to battery/electric operation by Clayton Equipment Ltd. The red stripe, presumably referencing the LU roundel, is a recent addition.

Opposite Rail Adhesion Car 6036 has performed leaf-clearing duties on the Metropolitan Line for many years but is likely to be replaced by a converted D Stock in the near future. When not formed involved with rail adhesion duties the car is stored in Neasden depot, as seen here.

Opposite The first of two five-car D Stock Rail Adhesion Trains undergoes trials on the South Ealing test track. The leaf-clearing equipment is sited on the centre car. The unit carries a modified corporate LU livery with the former passenger doors no longer painted red.

LU ENGINEERS' VEHICLE LIST

BATTERY LOCOMOTIVES 29

No.	Delivered	Builder	No.	Delivered	Builder
L15†	1970	Metro-Cammell	L30*	1965	Metro-Cammell
L16*†	1970	Metro-Cammell	L31*	1965	Metro-Cammell
L17*†	1971	Metro-Cammell	L32*	1965	Metro-Cammell
L18*†	1971	Metro-Cammell	L44*†	1974	BREL Doncaster
L19*†	1971	Metro-Cammell	L45*†	1974	BREL Doncaster
L20 †	1964	Metro-Cammell	L46*†	1974	BREL Doncaster
L21 †	1964	Metro-Cammell	L47†	1974	BREL Doncaster
L22*	1965	Metro-Cammell	L48†	1974	BREL Doncaster
L23*	1965	Metro-Cammell	L49*†	1974	BREL Doncaster
L24*	1965	Metro-Cammell	L50*†	1974	BREL Doncaster
L25*	1965	Metro-Cammell	L51*†	1974	BREL Doncaster
L26*	1965	Metro-Cammell	L52†	1974	BREL Doncaster
L27*	1965	Metro-Cammell	L53*†	1974	BREL Doncaster
L28*	1965	Metro-Cammell	L54†	1974	BREL Doncaster
L29*	1965	Metro-Cammell			

* Modified cabs ends.
† Fitted with Central Line ATP equipment.

BATTERY/DIESEL LOCOMOTIVES 14

No.	Delivered	Builder	No.	Delivered	Builder
1 *Britta Lotta* *	1996	Schöma	8 *Emma* ‡	1996	Schöma
2 *Nikki* †‡	1996	Schöma	9 *Debora*	1996	Schöma
3 *Claire* †	1996	Schöma	10 *Clementine* ‡	1996	Schöma
4 *Pam* ‡	1996	Schöma	11 *Joan* ‡	1996	Schöma
5 *Sophie* *‡	1996	Schöma	12 *Melanie*	1996	Schöma
6 *Denise* ‡	1996	Schöma	13 *Michele* ‡	1996	Schöma
7 *Anne Marie* ‡	1996	Schöma	14 *Carol* ‡	1996	Schöma

* Fitted with Wedgelock auto-coupler.
† Fitted with Wedgelock auto-coupler adaptor.
‡ Converted to battery/electric operation by Clayton Equipment Ltd at Ruislip.

HIGH-DECK WAGONS (40 TONNES CAPACITY) 6
Built 1987 by Procor, fitted with buckeye couplers.

HD871 *	HD872	HD873	HD874	HD875 *	HD876

* Fitted with hand-operated winch units.

GENERAL PURPOSE WAGONS (30 TONNES CAPACITY) 41
Built 1985 by Procor.

GP901 ‡	GP907	GP912	GP917	GP922	GP927	GP932	GP937
GP902	GP908 *	GP913	GP918	GP923	GP928	GP933 †	GP938
GP903	GP909	GP914	GP919	GP924	GP929 †	GP934	GP939
GP904	GP910	GP915	GP920	GP925 †	GP930	GP935	GP940
GP905	GP911	GP916	GP921	GP926 †	GP931	GP936	GP941
GP906							

* Fitted with equipment for weedkilling. Operates between battery locomotives.
† Fitted with cable turntables.
‡ Fitted with Roll Loader Crane.

FORMER CEMENT MIXER/MATCH WAGONS 12
Built 1987 by Procor, fitted with buckeye couplers.

CM950	CM952	CM954	MW956	MW958	MW960
CM951	CM953	CM955	MW957	MW959	MW961

Four wagons form two 'Tubevac' (ballast-sucker) trains in the formation CM951-CM955 and CM954-MW958. Each pair operates with a general purpose wagon (JLE1 and JLE2). CM951 and CM954 contain the diesel units, while CM955 and MW958 contain the ballast-sucking equipment. MW959-MW960 and MW956-MW961 operate as pairs.

CABLE WELL WAGONS 3
Built 1996 by Bombardier.

CW1053   CW1054   CW1055

GENERAL PURPOSE WAGONS 15
Built 1994 by Bombardier.

| JLE1 * | JLE3 * | JLE5 | JLE7 | JLE9 | JLE11 | JLE13 | JLE15 |
| JLE2 * | JLE4 | JLE6 | JLE8 | JLE10 | JLE12 | JLE14 | |

* Fitted with Palfinger crane to operate with CM954-MW958 (JLE2) and CM951-CM955 (JLE1).

BOGIE WELL WAGONS 4
Built 1994 by Bombardier.

JLE16 (d)   JLE17   JLE18   JLE19

(d) Fitted with de-icing equipment.

4-WHEEL CABLE DRUM WAGONS 4
Built 1994 by Bombardier.

JLE20   JLE21   JLE22   JLE23

SPOIL AND BALLAST WAGONS (34 TONNES CAPACITY) 60
Built 1982-1988 variously by BR Shildon and Swindon, and RFS Doncaster. Converted by ABB Crewe in 1995. SB231-239 have 'long' drawgear, SB 240-290 'short' drawgear.

No.	Former DB No.	No.	Former DB No.	No.	Former DB No.	No	Former DB No.
SB231	978865	SB246	978901	SB261	978051	SB276	978688
SB232	978047	SB247	978628	SB262	978076	SB277	978773
SB233	978916	SB248	978003	SB263	978086	SB278	978783
SB234	978864	SB249	978614	SB264	978145	SB279	978787
SB235	978820	SB250	978700	SB265	978161	SB280	978797
SB236	978702	SB251	978753	SB266	978211	SB281	978808
SB237	978677	SB252	978884	SB267	978318	SB282	978810
SB238	987788	SB253	978767	SB268	978408	SB283	978824
SB239	978809	SB254	978143	SB269	978420	SB284	978830
SB240	978647	SB255	978886	SB270	978608	SB285	978846
SB241	978652	SB256	978653	SB271	978617	SB286	978858
SB242	978766	SB257	978626	SB272	978669	SB287	978869
SB243	978897	SB258	978016	SB273	978678	SB288	978892
SB244	978898	SB259	978026	SB274	978682	SB289	978895
SB245	978088	SB260	978028	SB275	978685	SB290	978918

BOGIE HOPPER WAGONS (30 TONNES CAPACITY) 22
Built 1981 by W. H. Davis & Sons.

HW201	HW204	HW207	HW210	HW213	HW216	HW219	HW222
HW202	HW205	HW208	HW211	HW214	HW217	HW220	
HW203	HW206	HW209	HW212	HW215	HW218	HW221	

RAIL WAGONS (20 TONNES CAPACITY) 29
Built 1986 by Procor, fitted with buckeye couplers.

RW495*	RW802	RW806‡	RW810	RW814	RW818‡	RW822$	RW826$
RW505	RW803†	RW807	RW811	RW815(d)	RW819‡	RW823$	
RW506	RW804†	RW808	RW812	RW816(d)	RW820(d)	RW824$	
RW801†	RW805‡	RW809	RW813	RW817(d)	RW821‡	RW825$	

*   Fitted with End Unloading Unit.
†   Fitted with ELK Cranes.
‡   Fitted with End Loading Unit.
$ Forms part of the Long Welded Rail Train.
(d) Fitted with de-icing equipment .

TRACK MAINTENANCE MACHINES 6

No.	Date	Builder
TMM771†	1980	Plasser Theurer PU0716 Plain Line Tamping Machine
TMM772	1980	Plasser Theurer PU0716 Plain Line Tamping Machine
TMM773[1]	1980	Plasser Theurer PU0716 Plain Line Tamping Machine
TMM774	2007	Franz Plasser Points & Crossings Tamping Machine
TMM775	2015	Matisa Plain Line and Points & Crossings Tamping Machine
TMM776	2015	Matisa Plain Line and Points & Crossings Tamping Machine

Fitted with Central Line ATP equipment.
[1] Named *Alan Jenkins*

DIESEL-HYDRAULIC CRANES 8

No.	Date	Builder	Type
C623	1982	Cowan Sheldon	7.5 tonne crane (single jib)
C624	1984	Cowan Sheldon	7.5 tonne crane (single jib)
C625	1984	Cowan Sheldon	7.5 tonne crane (single jib)
C626	1984	Cowan Sheldon	7.5 tonne crane (single jib)
TRM627	1986	Cowan Sheldon	10 tonne Track Relaying Machine (twin jib), formerly numbered DHC627
TRM628	1993	Cowan Boyd	10 tonne Track Relaying Machine (twin jib), formerly numbered DHC628
TBA	2017	Kirov	25 tonne crane
TBA	2017	Kirov	25 tonne crane

CONCRETE MIXING AND DISTRIBUTION UNIT I

Ex-Rail and Sleeper Delivery Train, converted 2016 by Blend Plants, Italy

CM932

TRACK RECORDING TRAIN I

Ex-Central and Piccadilly Line 1960/1973 Tube Stock.

Ex-1960 Tube Stock DM 3901	Ex-1973 Tube Stock T 514	Ex-1960 Tube Stock DM 3905
Pilot car	Track Recording Vehicle	Pilot car
L132	TRC666	L133

ASSET INSPECTION TRAIN I

Ex-Victoria and Northern Line 1967/1972 Tube Stock.

DM(A)	T	DM(D)	DM(A)	T	DM(D)
3213	4213	3179	3079	4313	3313

RAIL ADHESION TRAINS 5

Ex-Metropolitan Line A Stock.

DM(A)	T	RAT	T	DM(D)
5110	6110	6036	6111	5111

Ex-District Line D Stock.

DM(A)	UNDM	RAT	UNDM	DM(D)
7010	8123	17010	8010	7123
7040	8107	17040	8040	7107

Ex-Central Line 1962 Tube Stock.

DM(A)	NDM	T	NDM	DM(D)
1570	9691	2440	9441	1441

Ex-Central Line 1962 Tube Stock.

DM(A)	T	NDM	DM(D)	DM(A)	NDM	T	DM(D)
1406	2682	9125	1681	1682	9577	2406	1407

TRAINING/FILMING TRAIN I

Ex-Northern Line 1972 MkI Tube Stock.

DM(A)	T	T	DM(D)
3229	4229	4329	3329

AFTERLIFE

Some former London Underground stock remains in service elsewhere. There are also a number of examples on various preserved railways and a few in private ownership. The London Transport Museum is another place to see old Underground cars, both at Covent Garden and in the Acton 'Depot' store.

ALDERNEY (Channel Islands)

The Alderney Railway, which opened in 1847, is one of the oldest and least-known railway lines in the British Isles. It was constructed by the British Government to convey stone from the eastern end of the Island to build the breakwater and the Victorian forts. Since 1980 passenger services have been run by the Alderney Railway Society, currently using a diesel locomotive hauling two 1959 Tube Stock cars (numbered 1044 and 1045) which had formed part of the Northern Line 'Heritage Train' painted in 1920s red and cream LER livery. The cars were acquired in 2001 to replace two 1938 Tube Stock cars that had succumbed to the salty sea air.

The Alderney Railway's two diesel-hauled 1959 Tube Stock DM cars are used on a mostly coastal route between Braye Road and Mannez Quarry & Lighthouse.

CLASS 230

The Class 230 or D-train is a project by Vivarail to convert redundant ex-LU D Stock cars to diesel-electric operation for use on regional rail lines within the United Kingdom. The concept retains the existing aluminium car bodies, traction motors and bogies, but with new Ford Duratorq diesel engines powering underfloor generator sets. Braking is rheostatic and dynamic and the Wedgelock couplers are retained. Production trains will be available in two- or three-car form with a choice of interior fittings including a universal access toilet. A three-car prototype unit has been produced and is designated Class 230 with the unit number of 230001. Formation is DMSO(A)-TSO-DMSO(B) and made up of former cars 7058, 17128 and 7511. Test-running in passenger service began in 2016 between Coventry and Nuneaton but an underfloor fire in the December of that year caused the cancellation of the trial. More recent developments are that 70 three-car trains are to be produced for use on the Wales & Borders franchise and these will have an option of being powered by battery packs instead of diesel engines. Over 200 cars are currently in store at Long Marston in connection with the D-train project.

The prototype Class 230 D-train conversion has resulted in extensive modifications of the cab fronts designed to increase crash-worthiness. Unit 230001 first carried passengers in June 2017 on a shuttle service between Honeybourne station and the Quinton Rail Technology Centre.

D-train interior showing the option of retaining a traditional LU mixed transverse/longitudinal low-backed seat layout.

An alternative internal layout available is 2+2 high-backed transverse seats with tables.

Also offered is the option of a RVAR-compliant toilet compartment.

Former trailer car 17128 with passenger doors now reduced from four to two.

ISLE OF WIGHT

Five trains of ex-LU 1938 Tube Stock remain in use by the Island Line rail franchise on the Isle of Wight. This line runs from Ryde Pier Head southwards for 8½ miles (13.7 km) to Shanklin and was electrified at 630V DC on the third-rail in 1967, when the remainder of the island's rail system was closed. The low headroom in Ryde Tunnel means that rolling stock of standard height cannot be used and initially ex-LT Standard Stock dating from between 1923 and 1934 was operated by BR as Classes 485 and 486 (or '4-VEC' and '3-TIS'). When these finally became life-expired, redundant 1938 Tube Stock was converted to replace them between 1989 and 1992 and designated Class 483. As well as modification to operate from the third rail only they were reformed into two-car units comprising DM cars only and identified as DMSO(A) and DMSO(B). Trains originally carried NSE livery, then a 'dinosaur' scheme, and are now in LT red, albeit with yellow warning ends. The South Western franchise passed from Stagecoach to FirstGroup/MTR in August 2017 and the new operator announced that the majority of existing rolling stock would be replaced. This did not include the Island Line trains however, which are now nearly 80 years' old.

Two-car 1938 Tube Stock unit 483004 at Ryde Pier Head on an evening Island Line service to Shanklin.

1938 Tube Stock unit 483007 crossing Ryde Pier.

The interiors of the Island Line trains are now more reminiscent of the 1956/59/62 Tube Stock family with extensive areas of grey. Note the PDC buttons and that additional heaters have been fitted at floor level.

UNIT FORMATIONS

S8 STOCK (METROPOLITAN LINE)

DM (A)	M1	M2	MS	MS	M2	M1	DM (D)
21002	22002	25002(d)	24002	24001	23001	22001	21001
21004	22004	25004(d)	24004	24003	23003	22003	21003
21006	22006	25006(d)	24006	24005	23005	22005	21005
21008	22008	25008(d)	24008	24007	23007	22007	21007
21010	22010	25010(d)	24010	24009	23009	22009	21009
21012	22012	25012(d)	24012	24011	23011	22011	21011
21014	22014	25014(d)	24014	24013	23013	22013	21013
21016	22016	25016(d)	24016	24015	23015	22015	21015
21018	22018	25018(d)	24018	24017	23017	22017	21017
21020	22020	25020(d)	24020	24019	23019	22019	21019
21022	22022	25022(d)	24022	24021	23021	22021	21021
21024	22024	25024(d)	24024	24023	23023	22023	21023
21026	22026	25026(d)	24026	24025	23025	22025	21025
21028	22028	25028(d)	24028	24027	23027	22027	21027
21030	22030	25030(d)	24030	24029	23029	22029	21029
21032	22032	25032(d)	24032	24031	23031	22031	21031
21034	22034	25034(d)	24034	24033	23033	22033	21033
21036	22036	25036(d)	24036	24035	23035	22035	21035
21038	22038	25038(d)	24038	24037	23037	22037	21037
21040	22040	25040(d)	24040	24039	23039	22039	21039
21042	22042	25042(d)	24042	24041	23041	22041	21041
21044	22044	25044(d)	24044	24043	23043	22043	21043
21046	22046	25046(d)	24046	24045	23045	22045	21045
21048	22048	25048(d)	24048	24047	23047	22047	21047
21050	22050	25050(d)	24050	24049	23049	22049	21049
21052	22052	25052(d)	24052	24051	23051	22051	21051
21054	22054	25054(d)	24054	24053	23053	22053	21053
21056	22056	25056(d)	24056	24055	23055	22055	21055
21058	22058	23058	24058	24057	23057	22057	21057
21060	22060	23060	24060	24059	23059	22059	21059
21062	22062	23062	24062	24061	23061	22061	21061
21064	22064	23064	24064	24063	23063	22063	21063
21066	22066	23066	24066	24065	23065	22065	21065
21068	22068	23068	24068	24067	23067	22067	21067
21070	22070	23070	24070	24069	23069	22069	21069
21072	22072	23072	24072	24071	23071	22071	21071
21074	22074	23074	24074	24073	23073	22073	21073
21076	22076	23076	24076	24075	23075	22075	21075
21078	22078	23078	24078	24077	23077	22077	21077
21080	22080	23080	24080	24079	23079	22079	21079
21082	22082	23082	24082	24081	23081	22081	21081
21084	22084	23084	24084	24083	23083	22083	21083
21086	22086	23086	24086	24085	23085	22085	21085
21088	22088	23088	24088	24087	23087	22087	21087
21090	22090	23090	24090	24089	23089	22089	21089
21092	22092	23092	24092	24091	23091	22091	21091
21094	22094	23094	24094	24093	23093	22093	21093
21096	22096	23096	24096	24095	23095	22095	21095
21098	22098	23098	24098	24097	23097	22097	21097
21100[1]	22100	23100	24100	24099	23099	22099	21099
21102	22102	23102	24102	24101	23101	22101	21101
21104	22104	23104	24104	24103	23103	22103	21103
21106	22106	23106	24106	24105	23105	22105	21105
21108	22108	23108	24108	24107	23107	22107	21107
21110	22110	23110	24110	24109	23109	22109	21109
21112	22112	23112	24112	24111	23111	22111	21111
21114	22114	23114	24114	24113	23113	22113	21113
21116	22116	23116	24116	24115	23115	22115	21115

[1] – Named *Tim O'Toole CBE*

S7 STOCK (CIRCLE, DISTRICT AND HAMMERSMITH & CITY LINES)

DM (A)	M1	M2	MS	MS	M1	DM (D)
21302	22302	25302(d)	24302	24301	22301	21301¹
21304	22304	25304(d)	24304	24303	22303	21303
21306	22306	25306(d)	24306	24305	22305	21305
21308	22308	25308(d)	24308	24307	22307	21307
21310	22310	25310(d)	24310	24309	22309	21309
21312	22312	25312(d)	24312	24311	22311	21311
21314	22314	25314(d)	24314	24313	22313	21313
21316	22316	25316(d)	24316	24315	22315	21315
21318	22318	25318(d)	24318	24317	22317	21317
21320	22320	25320(d)	24320	24319	22319	21319
21322	22322	25322(d)	24322	24321	22321	21321
21324*	22324	25324(d)	24324	24323	22323	21323
21326	22326	25326(d)	24326	24325	22325	21325
21328*	22328	25328(d)	24328	24327	22327	21327
21330	22330	25330(d)	24330	24329	22329	21329
21332	22332	25332(d)	24332	24331	22331	21331
21334	22334	25334(d)	24334	24333	22333	21333
21336	22336	25336(d)	24336	24335	22335	21335
21338	22338	25338(d)	24338	24337	22337	21337
21340	22340	25340(d)	24340	24339	22339	21339
21342	22342	25342(d)	24342	24341	22341	21341
21344	22344	25344(d)	24344	24343	22343	21343
21346	22346	25346(d)	24346	24345	22345	21345
21348	22348	25348(d)	24348	24347	22347	21347
21350	22350	25350(d)	24350	24349	22349	21349
21352	22352	25352(d)	24352	24351	22351	21351
21354	22354	25354(d)	24354	24353	22353	21353
21356	22356	25356(d)	24356	24355	22355	21355
21358	22358	25358(d)	24358	24357	22357	21357
21360	22360	25360(d)	24360	24359	22359	21359
21362	22362	25362(d)	24362	24361	22361	21361
21364	22364	25364(d)	24364	24363	22363	21363
21366	22366	25366(d)	24366	24365	22365	21365
21368	22368	25368(d)	24368	24367	22367	21367
21370	22370	25370(d)	24370	24369	22369	21369
21372	22372	25372(d)	24372	24371	22371	21371
21374	22374	25374(d)	24374	24373	22373	21373
21376	22376	25376(d)	24376	24375	22375	21375
21378	22378	25378(d)	24378	24377	22377	21377
21380	22380	25380(d)	24380	24379	22379	21379
21382	22382	25382(d)	24382	24381	22381	21381
21384	22384	23384	24384	24383	22383	21383
21386	22386	23386	24386	24385	22385	21385
21388	22388	23388	24388	24387	22387	21387
21390	22390	23390	24390	24389	22389	21389
21392	22392	23392	24392	24391	22391	21391
21394	22394	23394	24394	24393	22393	21393
21396	22396	23396	24396	24395	22395	21395
21398	22398	23398	24398	24397	22397	21397
21400	22400	23400	24400	24399	22399	21399
21402	22402	23402	24402	24401	22401	21401
21404	22404	23404	24404	24403	22403	21403
21406	22406	23406	24406	24405	22405	21405
21408	22408	23408	24408	24407	22407	21407
21410	22410	23410	24410	24409	22409	21409
21412	22412	23412	24412	24411	22411	21411
21414	22414	23414	24414	24413	22413	21413
21416	22416	23416	24416	24415	22415	21415
21418	22418	23418	24418	24417	22417	21417
21420	22420	23420	24420	24419	22419	21419

21422	22422	23422	24422	24421	22421	21421
21424	22424	23424	24424	24423	22423	21423
21426	22426	23426	24426	24425	22425	21425
21428	22428	23428	24428	24427	22427	21427
21430	22430	23430	24430	24429	22429	21429
21432	22432	23432	24432	24431	22431	21431
21434	22434	23434	24434	24433	22433	21433
21436	22436	23436	24436	24435	22435	21435
21438	22438	23438	24438	24437	22437	21437
21440	22440	23440	24440	24439	22439	21439
21442	22442	23442	24442	24441	22441	21441
21444	22444	23444	24444	24443	22443	21443
21446	22446	23446	24446	24445	22445	21445
21448	22448	23448	24448	24447	22447	21447
21450	22450	23450	24450	24449	22449	21449
21452	22452	23452	24452	24451	22451	21451
21454	22454	23454	24454	24453	22453	21453
21456	22456	23456	24456	24455	22455	21455
21458	22458	23458	24458	24457	22457	21457
21460	22460	23460	24460	24459	22459	21459
21462	22462	23462	24462	24461	22461	21461
21464	22464	23464	24464	24463	22463	21463
21466	22466	23466	24466	24465	22465	21465
21468	22468	23468	24468	24467	22467	21467
21470	22470	23470	24470	24469	22469	21469
21472	22472	23472	24472	24471	22471	21471
21474	22474	23474	24474	24473	22473	21473
21476	22476	23476	24476	24475	22475	21475
21478	22478	23478	24478	24477	22477	21477
21480	22480	23480	24480	24479	22479	21479
21482	22482	23482	24482	24481	22481	21481
21484	22484	23484	24484	24483	22483	21483
21486	22486	23486	24486	24485	22485	21485
21488	22488	23488	24488	24487	22487	21487
21490	22490	23490	24490	24489	22489	21489
21492	22492	23492	24492	24491	22491	21491
21494	22494	23494	24494	24493	22493	21493
21496	22496	23496	24496	24495	22495	21495
21498	22498	23498	24498	24497	22497	21497
21500	22500	23500	24500	24499	22499	21499
21502	22502	23502	24502	24501	22501	21501
21504	22504	23504	24504	24503	22503	21503
21506	22506	23506	24506	24505	22505	21505
21508	22508	23508	24508	24507	22507	21507
21510	22510	23510	24510	24509	22509	21509
21512	22512	23512	24512	24511	22511	21511
21514	22514	23514	24514	24513	22513	21513
21516	22516	23516	24516	24515	22515	21515
21518	22518	23518	24518	24517	22517	21517
21520	22520	23520	24520	24519	22519	21519
21522	22522	23522	24522	24521	22521	21521
21524	22524	23524	24524	24523	22523	21523
21526	22526	23526	24526	24525	22525	21525
21528	22528	23528	24528	24527	22527	21527
21530	22530	23530	24530	24529	22529	21529
21532	22532	23532	24532	24531	22531	21531
21534	22534	23534	24534	24533	22533	21533
21536	22536	23536	24536	24535	22535	21535
21538	22538	23538	24538	24537	22537	21537
21540	22540	23540	24540	24539	22539	21539
21542	22542	23542	24542	24541	22541	21541
21544	22544	23544	24544	24543	22543	21543
21546	22546	23546	24546	24545	22545	21545
21548	22548	23548	24548	24547	22547	21547

21550	22550	23550	24550	24549	22549	21549
21552	22552	23552	24552	24551	22551	21551
21554	22554	23554	24554	24553	22553	21553
21556	22556	23556	24556	24555	22555	21555
21558	22558	23558	24558	24557	22557	21557
21560	22560	23560	24560	24559	22559	21559
21562	22562	23562	24562	24561	22561	21561
21564	22564	23564	24564	24563	22563	21563
21566	22566	23566	24566	24565	22565	21565

(d) Fitted with de-icing equipment.
* Units temporary formed as 8 cars for short-term service on the Metropolitan Line:
21324-22324-25324-24324-24323-25384-22323-21323
21328-22328-25328-24328-24327-25386-22327-21327
[1] – Named *Queen Elizabeth II*

1972 MKII TUBE STOCK (BAKERLOO LINE)

4-CAR 'A'-END UNITS

DM SOUTH LEADING	TRAILER	TRAILER	DM NORTH MIDDLE
3231	4231	4331	3331
3232	4232	4332	3332
3233	4233	4333	3333
3234	4234	4334	3334
3235	4235	4335	3335
3236	4236	4336	3336
3237	4237	4337	3337
3238	4238	4338	3338
3239	4239	4339	3339
3240	4240	4340	3340
3241	4241	4341	3341
3242	4242	4342	3342
3243	4243	4343	3343
3244	4244	4344	3344
3245	4245	4345	3345
3246	4246	4346	3346
3247	4247	4347	3347
3248	4248	4348	3348
3250	4250	4350	3350
3251	4251	4351	3351
3252	4252	4352(d)	3352
3253	4253	4353(d)	3353
3254	4254	4354(d)	3354
3255	4255	4355(d)	3355
3256	4256	4356(d)	3356
3258	4258	4358(d)	3358
3259	4259	4359(d)	3359
3260	4260	4360(d)	3360
3261	4261	4361(d)	3361
3262	4262	4362(d)	3362
3263	4263	4363(d)	3363
3264*	4264*	4364*	3364*
3265*	4265*	4365*	3365*
3266*	4266*	4366†	3366†
3267*	4267*	4367*	3367*

DM SOUTH LEADING	TRAILER	TRAILER	UNDM NORTH MIDDLE
3299†	4299†	4399†	3399†

3-CAR 'D' END UNITS

UNDM SOUTH MIDDLE	TRAILER	DM NORTH LEADING
3431	4531	3531
3432	4532	3532
3433	4533	3533
3434	4534	3534
3435	4535	3535
3436	4536	3536
3437	4537	3537
3438	4538	3538
3440	4540	3540
3441	4541	3541
3442	4542	3542
3443	4543	3543
3444	4544	3544
3445	4545	3545
3446	4546	3546
3447	4547	3547
3448	4548	3548
3449	4549	3549
3450	4550	3550
3451	4551	3551
3452	4552	3552
3453	4553	3553
3454	4554	3554
3455	4555	3555
3456	4556	3556
3457	4557	3557
3458	4558	3558
3459	4559	3559
3460	4560	3560
3461	4561	3561
3462	4562	3562
3463	4563	3563
3464*	4564*	3564*
3465*	4565*	3565*
3466*	4566*	3566*
3467*	4567*	3567*

(d) Fitted with de-icing equipment.
* 1972 MkI Stock cars renumbered.
† 1972 MkII Stock cars renumbered.

1973 TUBE STOCK (PICCADILLY LINE)

DM 'A'-END WEST LEADING	TRAILER	UNDM 'D'-END EAST MIDDLE	UNDM 'A'-END WEST MIDDLE	TRAILER	DM 'D'-END EAST LEADING
100	500	300	301	501	101
102	502	302	303	503	103
104	504	304	305	505	105
106	506	306	307	507	107
108	508	308	309	509	109
110	510	310	311	511	111
112	512	312	313	513	113
116	516	316	315	515	115
118	518	318	317	517	117
120	520	320	319	519	119
122	522	322	321	521	121
124	524	324	323	523	123
126	526	326	325	525	125
128	528	328	327	527	127
130	530	330	329	529	129
132	532	332	331	531	131
134	534	334	333	533	133
136	536	336	335	535	135
138	538	338	337	537	137
140	540	340	339	539	139
142	542	342	341	541	141
144	544	344	343	543	143
146	546	346	345	545	145
148	548	348	347	547	147
150	550	350	349	549	149
152	552	352	351	551	151
154	554	354	353	553	153
156	556	356	355	555	155
158	558	358	357	557	157
160	560	360	359	559	159
162	562	362	361	561	161
164	564	364	363	563	163
168	568	368	365	565	165
170	570	370	367	567	167
172	572	372	369	569	169
174	574	374	371	571	171
176	576	376	373	573	173
178	578	378	375	575	175
180	580	380	377	577	177
182	582	382	379	579	179
184	584	384	381	581	181
186	586	386	383	583	183
188	588	388	385	585	185
190	590	390	387	587	187
192	592	392	389	589	189
194	594	394	391	591	191
196	596	396	393	593	193
198	598	398	395	595	195

DM 'A'-END WEST LEADING	TRAILER	UNDM 'D'-END EAST MIDDLE	UNDM 'A'-END WEST MIDDLE	TRAILER	DM 'D'-END EAST LEADING
200	600	400	397	597	197
202	602	402	399	599	199
206	606(d)	406	401	601	201
208	608(d)	408	403	603	203
210	610(d)	410	405	605	205
212	612(d)	412	407	607	207
214	614(d)	414	409	609	209
216	616(d)	416	411	611	211
218	618(d)	418	413	613	213
220	620(d)	420	415	615	215
222	622(d)	422	417	617	217
224	624(d)	424	419	619	219
226	626(d)	426	421	621	221
228	628(d)	428	423	623	223
230	630(d)	430	425	625	225
232	632(d)	432	427	627	227
234	634(d)	434	429	629	229
236	636(d)	436	431	631	231
238	638(d)	438	433	633	233
240	640(d)	440	435	635	235
242	642(d)	442	437	637	237
244	644(d)	444	439	639	239
246	644(d)	446	441	641	241
248	648(d)	448	443	643	243
250	650(d)	450	445	645	245
252	652(d)	452	447	647	247
			449	649	249
			451	651	251
			453	653	253

DOUBLE-ENDED UNITS

DM 'A'-END WEST	TRAILER	DM 'D'-END EAST	DM 'A'-END WEST	TRAILER	DM 'D'-END EAST
854	654	855	876	676	877
856	656	857	878	678	879
858	658	859	880	680	881
860	660	861	882	682	883
862	662	863	884	684	885
864	664	865	886	686	887
866	666	867	890	690	891
868	668	869	892	692	893
870	670	871	894	694	895
872	672	873	896*	696*	897*
874	674	875			

* Cars renumbered ex 114-688-889 respectively.
(d) Fitted with de-icing equipment.

1992 TUBE STOCK TWO-CAR 'A' - 'B' UNITS (CENTRAL LINE)

DM 'A' CAR	NDM 'B' CAR	DM 'A' CAR	NDM 'B' CAR	DM 'A' CAR	NDM 'B' CAR	DM 'A' CAR	NDM 'B' CAR
91001	92001	91089	92089	91177	92177	91265	92265
91003	92003	91091	92091	91179	92179	91267	92267
91005	92005	91093	92093	91181	92181	91269	92269
91007	92007	91095	92095	91183	92183	91271	92271
91009	92009	91097	92097	91185	92185	91273	92273
91011	92011	91099	92099	91187	92187	91275	92275
91013	92013	91101	92101	91189	92189	91277	92277
91015	92015	91103	92103	91191	92191	91279	92279
91017	92017	91105	92105	91193	92193	91281	92281
91019	92019	91107	92107	91195	92195	91283	92283
91021	92021	91109	92109	91197	92197	91285	92285
91023	92023	91111	92111	91199	92199	91287	92287
91025	92025	91113	92113	91201	92201	91289	92289
91027	92027	91115	92115	91203	92203	91291	92291
91029	92029	91117	92117	91205	92205	91293	92293
91031	92031	91119	92119	91207	92207	91295	92295
91033	92033	91121	92121	91209	92209	91297	92297
91035	92035	91123	92123	91211	92211	91299	92299
91037	92037	91125	92125	91213	92213	91301	92301
91039	92039	91127	92127	91215	92215	91303	92303
91041	92041	91129	92129	91217	92217	91305	92305
91043	92043	91131	92131	91219	92219	91307	92307
91045	92045	91133	92133	91221	92221	91309	92309
91047	92047	91135	92135	91223	92223	91311	92311
91049	92049	91137	92137	91225	92225	91313	92313
91051	92051	91139	92139	91227	92227	91315	92315
91053	92053	91141	92141	91229	92229	91317	92317
91055	92055	91143	92143	91231	92231	91319	92319
91057	92057	91145	92145	91233	92233	91321	92321
91059	92059	91147	92147	91235	92235	91323	92323
91061	92061	91149	92149	91237	92237	91325	92325
91063	92063	91151	92151	91239	92239	91327	92327
91065	92065	91153	92153	91241	92241	91329	92329
91067	92067	91155	92155	91243	92243	91331	92331
91069	92069	91157	92157	91245	92245	91333	92333
91071	92071	91159	92159	91247	92247	91335	92335
91073	92073	91161	92161	91249	92249	91337	92337
91075	92075	91163	92163	91251	92251	91339	92339
91077	92077	91165	92165	91253	92253	91341	92341
91079	92079	91167	92167	91255	92255	91343	92343
91081	92081	91169	92169	91257	92257	91345	92345
91083	92083	91171	92171	91259	92259	91347	92347
91085	92085	91173	92173	91261	92261	91349	92349
91087	92087	91175	92175	91263	92263		

1992 TUBE STOCK TWO-CAR 'B' - 'C' UNITS

NDM 'B' CAR	NDM 'C' CAR	NDM 'B' CAR	NDM 'C' CAR	NDM 'B' CAR	NDM 'C' CAR	NDM 'B' CAR	NDM 'C' CAR
92002	93002	92070	93070	92138	93138	92206	93206
92004	93004	92072	93072	92140	93140	92208	93208
92006	93006	92074	93074	92142	93142	92210	93210
92008	93008	92076	93076	92144	93144	92212	93212
92010	93010	92078	93078	92146	93146	92214	93214
92012	93012	92080	93080	92148	93148	92216	93216
92014	93014	92082	93082	92150	93150	92218	93218
92016	93016	92084	93084	92152	93152	92220	93220
92018	93018	92086	93086	92154	93154	92222	93222
92020	93020	92088	93088	92156	93156	92224	93224
92022	93022	92090	93090	92158	93158	92226	93226
92024	93024	92092	93092	92160	93160	92228	93228
92026	93026	92094	93094	92162	93162	92230	93230
92028	93028	92096	93096	92164	93164	92232	93232
92030	93030	92098	93098	92166	93166	92234	93234
92032	93032	92100	93100	92168	93168	92236	93236
92034	93034	92102	93102	92170	93170	92238	93238
92036	93036	92104	93104	92172	93172	92240	93240
92038	93038	92106	93106	92174	93174	92242	93242
92040	93040	92108	93108	92176	93176	92244	93244
92042	93042	92110	93110	92178	93178	92246	93246
92044	93044	92112	93112	92180	93180	92248	93248
92046	93046	92114	93114	92182	93182	92250	93250
92048	93048	92116	93116	92184	93184	92252	93252
92050	93050	92118	93118	92186	93186	92254	93254
92052	93052	92120	93120	92188	93188	92256	93256
92054	93054	92122	93122	92190	93190	92258	93258
92056	93056	92124	93124	92192	93192	92260	93260
92058	93058	92126	93126	92194	93194	92262	93262
92060	93060	92128	93128	92196	93196	92264	93264
92062	93062	92130	93130	92198	93198	92266	93266
92064	93064	92132	93132	92200	93200		
92066	93066	92134	93134	92202	93202		
92068	93068	92136	93136	92204	93204		

1992 TUBE STOCK TWO-CAR 'B' - 'D' DE-ICING UNITS

NDM 'B' CAR	NDM 'D' CAR	NDM 'B' CAR	NDM 'D' CAR	NDM 'B' CAR	NDM 'D' CAR	NDM 'B' CAR	NDM 'D' CAR
92402	93402	92418	93418	92434	93434	92450	93450
92404	93404	92420	93420	92436	93436	92452	93452
92406	93406	92422	93422	92438	93438	92454	93454
92408	93408	92424	93424	92440	93440	92456	93456
92410	93410	92426	93426	92442	93442	92458	93458
92412	93412	92428	93428	92444	93444	92460	93460
92414	93414	92430	93430	92446	93446	92462	93462
92416	93416	92432	93432	92448	93448	92464	93464

1992 TUBE STOCK (WATERLOO & CITY LINE)

TWO-CAR 'E' - 'F' UNITS

DM	NDM	DM	NDM	DM	NDM	DM	NDM
65501	67501	65504	67504	65507	67507	65510	67510
65502	67502	65505	67505	65508	67508		
65503	67503	65506	67506	65509	67509		

1995 TUBE STOCK (NORTHERN LINE)

THREE-CAR 'D'-END UNITS

DM	TRAILER	UNDM MIDDLE
51501	52501	53501
51503	52503	53503
51505	52505	53505
51507	52507	53507
51509	52509	53509
51511	52511	53511
51513	52513	53513
51515	52515	53515
51517	52517	53517
51519	52519	53519
51521	52521	53521
51523	52523	53523
51525	52525	53525
51527	52527	53527
51529	52529	53529
51531	52531	53531
51533	52533	53533
51535	52535	53535
51537	52537	53537
51539	52539	53539
51541	52541	53541
51543	52543	53543
51545	52545	53545
51547	52547	53547
51549	52549	53549
51551	52551	53551
51553	52553	53553
51555	52555	53555
51557	52557	53557
51559	52559	53559
51561	52561	53561
51563	52563	53563
51565	52565	53565
51567	52567	53567
51569	52569	53569
51571	52571	53571
51573	52573	53573
51575	52575	53575
51577	52577	53577
51579	52579	53579
51581	52581	53581
51583	52583	53583
51585	52585	53585
51587	52587	53587
51589	52589	53589
51591	52591	53591
51593	52593	53593
51595	52595	53595
51597	52597	53597
51599	52599	53599
51601	52601	53601
51603	52603	53603
51605	52605	53605
51607	52607	53607
51609	52609	53609
51611	52611	53611

THREE-CAR 'A'-END UNITS

UNDM MIDDLE	TRAILER	DM
53502	52502	51502
53504	52504	51504
53506	52506	51506
53508	52508	51508
53510	52510	51510
53512	52512	51512
53514	52514	51514
53516	52516	51516
53518	52518	51518
53520	52520	51520
53522	52522	51522
53524	52524	51524
53526	52526	51526
53528	52528	51528
53530	52530	51530
53532	52532	51532
53534	52534	51534
53536	52536	51536
53538	52538	51538
53540	52540	51540
53542	52542	51542
53544	52544	51544
53546	52546	51546
53548	52548	51548
53550	52550	51550
53552	52552	51552
53554	52554	51554
53556	52556	51556
53558	52558	51558
53560	52560	51560
53562	52562	51562
53564	52564	51564
53566	52566	51566
53568	52568	51568
53570	52570	51570
53572	52572	51572
53574	52574	51574
53576	52576	51576
53578	52578	51578
53580	52580	51580
53582	52582	51582
53584	52584	51584
53586	52586	51586
53588	52588	51588
53590	52590	51590
53592	52592	51592
53594	52594	51594
53596	52596	51596
53598	52598	51598
53600	52600	51600
53602	52602	51602
53604	52604	51604
53606	52606	51606
53608	52608	51608
53610	52610	51610
53612	52612	51612

DM	TRAILER	UNDM MIDDLE
51613	52613	53613
51615	52615	53615
51617	52617	53617
51619	52619	53619
51621	52621	53621
51623	52623	53623
51625	52625	53625
51627	52627	53627
51629	52629	53629
51631	52631	53631
51633	52633	53633
51635	52635	53635
51637	52637	53637
51639	52639	53639
51641	52641	53641
51643	52643	53643
51645	52645	53645
51647	52647	53647
51649	52649	53649
51651	52651	53651
51653	52653	53653
51655	52655	53655
51657	52657	53657
51659	52659	53659
51661	52661	53661
51663	52663	53663
51665	52665	53665
51667	52667	53667
51669	52669	53669
51671	52671	53671
51673	52673	53673
51675	52675	53675
51677	52677	53677
51679	52679	53679
51681	52681	53681
51683	52683	53683
51685	52685	53685

UNDM MIDDLE	TRAILER	DM
53614	52614	51614
53616	52616	51616
53618	52618	51618
53620	52620	51620
53622	52622	51622
53624	52624	51624
53626	52626	51626
53628	52628	51628
53630	52630	51630
53632	52632	51632
53634	52634	51634
53636	52636	51636
53638	52638	51638
53640	52640	51640
53642	52642	51642
53644	52644	51644
53646	52646	51646
53648	52648	51648
53650	52650	51650
53652	52652	51652
53654	52654	51654
53656	52656	51656
53658	52658	51658
53660	52660	51660
53662	52662	51662
53664	52664	51664
53666	52666	51666
53668	52668	51668
53670	52670	51670
53672	52672	51672
53674	52674	51674
53676	52676	51676
53678	52678	51678
53680	52680	51680
53682	52682	51682
53684	52684	51684
53686	52686	51686

THREE-CAR 'D'-END DE-ICING UNITS

DM	DE-ICING TRAILER	UNDM MIDDLE
51701	52701	53701
51703	52703	53703
51705	52705	53705
51707	52707	53707
51709	52709	53709
51711	52711	53711
51713	52713	53713
51715	52715	53715
51717	52717	53717
51719	52719	53719
51721	52721	53721
51723	52723	53723
51725	52725	53725

THREE-CAR 'A'-END DE-ICING UNITS

UNDM MIDDLE	DE-ICING TRAILER	DM
53702	52702	51702
53704	52704	51704
53706	52706	51706
53708	52708	51708
53710	52710	51710
53712	52712	51712
53714	52714	51714
53716	52716	51716
53718	52718	51718
53720	52720	51720
53722	52722	51722
53724	52724	51724
53726	52726	51726

1996 TUBE STOCK (JUBILEE LINE)

| THREE-CAR 'A'-END UNITS | | | FOUR-CAR 'D'-END UNITS | | | |
DM WEST/NORTH	TRAILER	UNDM MIDDLE	UNDM MIDDLE	SPECIAL TRAILER	TRAILER	DM EAST/SOUTH
96002	96202	96402	96401	96601	96201	96001
96004	96204	96404	96403	96603	96203	96003
96006	96206	96406	96405	96605	96205	96005
96008	96208	96408	96407	96607	96207	96007
96010	96210	96410	96409	96609	96209	96009
96012	96212	96412	96411	96611	96211	96011
96014	96214	96414	96413	96613	96213	96013
96016	96216	96416	96415	96615	96215	96015
96018	96218	96418	96417	96617	96217	96017
96020	96220	96420	96419	96619	96219	96019
96022	96222	96422	96421	96621	96221	96021
96024	96224	96424	96423	96623	96223	96023
96026	96226	96426	96425	96625	96225	96025
96028	96228	96428	96427	96627	96227	96027
96030	96230	96430	96429	96629	96229	96029
96032	96232	96432	96431	96631	96231	96031
96034	96234	96434	96433	96633	96233	96033
96036	96236	96436	96435	96635	96235	96035
96038	96238	96438	96437	96637	96237	96037
96040	96240	96440	96439	96639	96239	96039
96042	96242	96442	96441	96641	96241	96041
96044	96244	96444	96443	96643	96243	96043
96046	96246	96446	96445	96645	96245	96045
96048	96248	96448	96447	96647	96247	96047
96050	96250	96450	96449	96649	96249	96049
96052	96252	96452	96451	96651	96251	96051
96054	96254	96454	96453	96653	96253	96053
96056	96256	96456	96455	96655	96255	96055
96058	96258	96458	96457	96657	96257	96057
96060	96260	96460	96459	96659	96259	96059
96062	96262	96462	96461	96661	96261	96061
96064	96264	96464	96463	96663	96263	96063

| THREE-CAR 'A'-END UNITS | | | FOUR-CAR 'D'-END UNITS | | | |
DM WEST/NORTH	TRAILER	UNDM MIDDLE	UNDM MIDDLE	SPECIAL TRAILER	TRAILER	DM EAST/SOUTH
96066	96266	96466	96465	96665	96265	96065
96068	96268	96468	96467	96667	96267	96067
96070	96270	96470	96469	96669	96269	96069
96072	96272	96472	96471	96671	96271	96071
96074	96274	96474	96473	96673	96273	96073
96076	96276	96476	96475	96675	96275	96075
96078	96278	96478	96477	96677	96277	96077
96080	96880(D)	96480	96479	96679	96279	96079
96082	96882(D)	96482	96481	96681	96281	96081
96084	96884(D)	96484	96483	96683	96283	96083
96086	96886(D)	96486	96485	96685	96285	96085
96088	96888(D)	96488	96487	96687	96287	96087
96090	96890(D)	96490	96489	96689	96289	96089
96092	96892(D)	96492	96491	96691	96291	96091
96094	96894(D)	96494	96493	96693	96293	96093
96096	96896(D)	96496	96495	96695	96295	96095
96098	96898(D)	96498	96497	96697	96297	96097
96100	96900(D)	96500	96499	96699	96299	96099
96102	96902(D)	96502	96501	96701	96301	96101
96104	96904(D)	96504	96503	96703	96303	96103
96106	96906(D)	96506	96505	96705	96305	96105
96108	96908(D)	96508	96507	96707	96307	96107
96110	96910(D)	96510	96509	96709	96309	96109
96112	96912(D)	96512	96511	96711	96311	96111
96114	96914(D)	96514	96513	96713	96313	96113
96116	96916(D)	96516	96515	96715	96315	96115
96118	96918(D)	96518	96517	96717	96317	96117
96120	96320	96520	96519	96719	96319	96119
96122	96322	96522	96521	96721	96321	96121
96124	96324	96524	96523	96723	96323	96123
96126	96326	96526	96525	96725	96325	96125

2009 TUBE STOCK (VICTORIA LINE)

A1 DM	B1 TRAILER	C1 NDM	D1 UNDM	D UNDM	C NDM	B TRAILER	A DM
11002	12002	13002	14002	14001	13001	12001	11001
11004	12004	13004	14004	14003	13003	12003	11003
11006	12006	13006	14006	14005	13005	12005	11005
11008	12008	13008	14008	14007	13007	12007	11007
11010	12010	13010	14010	14009	13009	12009	11009
11012	12012	13012	14012	14011	13011	12011	11011
11014	12014	13014	14014	14013	13013	12013	11013
11016	12016	13016	14016	14015	13015	12015	11015
11018	12018	13018	14018	14017	13017	12017	11017
11020	12020	13020	14020	14019	13019	12019	11019
11022	12022	13022	14022	14021	13021	12021	11021
11024	12024	13024	14024	14023	13023	12023	11023
11026	12026	13026	14026	14025	13025	12025	11025
11028	12028	13028	14028	14027	13027	12027	11027
11030	12030	13030	14030	14029	13029	12029	11029
11032	12032	13032	14032	14031	13031	12031	11031
11034	12034	13034	14034	14033	13033	12033	11033
11036	12036	13036	14036	14035	13035	12035	11035
11038	12038	13038	14038	14037	13037	12037	11037
11040	12040	13040	14040	14039	13039	12039	11039
11042	12042	13042	14042	14041	13041	12041	11041
11044	12044	13044	14044	14043	13043	12043	11043
11046	12046	13046	14046	14045	13045	12045	11045
11048	12048	13048	14048	14047	13047	12047	11047

A1 DM	B1 TRAILER	C1 NDM	D1 UNDM	D UNDM	C NDM	B TRAILER	A DM
11050	12050	13050	14050	14049	13049	12049	11049
11052	12052	13052	14052	14051	13051	12051	11051
11054	12054	13054	14054	14053	13053	12053	11053
11056	12056	13056	14056	14055	13055	12055	11055
11058	12058	13058	14058	14057	13057	12057	11057
11060	12060	13060	14060	14059	13059	12059	11059
11062	12062	13062	14062	14061	13061	12061	11061
11064	12064	13064	14064	14063	13063	12063	11063
11066	12066	13066	14066	14065	13065	12065	11065
11068	12068	13068	14068	14067	13067	12067	11067
11070	12070	13070	14070	14069	13069	12069	11069
11072	12072	13072	14072	14071	13071	12071	11071
11074	12074	13074	14074	14073	13073	12073	11073
11076	12076	13076	14076	14075	13075	12075	11075
11078	12078	13078	14078	14077	13077	12077	11077
11080	12080	13080	14080	14079	13079	12079	11079
11082	12082	13082	14082	14081	13081	12081	11081
11084	12084	13084	14084	14083	13083	12083	11083
11086	12086	13086	14086	14085	13085	12085	11085
11088	12088	13088	14088	14087	13087	12087	11087
11090	12090	13090	14090	14089	13089	12089	11089
11092	12092	13092	14092	14091	13091	12091	11091
11094	12094	13094	14094	14093	13093	12093	11093

LONDON OVERGROUND

GOSPEL OAK – BARKING LINE
CLASS 172/0

UNIT No.	DMSO	DMSO
172001	59311	59411
172002	59312	59412
172003	59313	59413
172004	59314	59414
172005	59315	59415
172006	59316	59416
172007	59317	59417
172008	59318	59418

CLASS 378/1 – DC

UNIT No.	DMSO	MSO	TSO	DMSO
378135	38035	38235	38335	38135
378136	38036	38236	38336	38136
378137	38037	38237	38337	38137
378138	38038	38238	38338	38138
378139	38039	38239	38339	38139
378140	38040	38240	38340	38140
378141	38041	38241	38341	38141
378142	38042	38242	38342	38142
378143	38043	38243	38343	38143
378144	38044	38244	38344	38144
378145	38045	38245	38345	38145
378146	38046	38246	38346	38146
378147	38047	38247	38347	38147
378148	38048	38248	38348	38148
378149	38049	38249	38349	38149
378150 (d)	38050	38250	38350	38150
378151 (d)	38051	38251	38351	38151
378152 (d)	38052	38252	38352	38152
378153 (d)	38053	38253	38353	38153
378154 (d)	38054	38254	38354	38154

(d) Fitted with de-icing equipment

CLASS 378/2 – AC/DC

UNIT No.	DMSO	MSO	PTSO	DMSO
378201	38001	38201	38301	38101
378202	38002	38202	38302	38102
378203	38003	38203	38303	38103
378204	38004[1]	38204	38304	38104
378205	38005	38205	38305	38105
378206	38006	38206	38306	38106
378207	38007	38207	38307	38107
378208	38008	38208	38308	38108
378209	38009	38209	38309	38109
378210	38010	38210	38310	38110
378211	38011	38211	38311	38111
378212	38012	38212	38312	38112
378213	38013	38213	38313	38113
378214	38014	38214	38314	38114
378215	38015	38215	38315	38115
378216 (d)	38016	38216	38316	38116
378217 (d)	38017	38217	38317	38117
378218 (d)	38018	38218	38318	38118
378219 (d)	38019	38219	38319	38119
378220 (d)	38020	38220	38320	38120
378221	38021	38221	38321	38121
378222	38022	38222	38322	38122
378223	38023	38223	38323	38123
378224	38024	38224	38324	38124
378225	38025	38225	38325	38125
378226	38026	38226	38326	38126
378227	38027	38227	38327	38127
378228	38028	38228	38328	38128
378229	38029	38229	38329	38129
378230	38030	38230	38330	38130
378231	38031	38231	38331	38131
378232	38032	38232	38332	38132
378233	38033[2]	38233	38333	38133
378234	38034	38234	38334	38134
378255	38055	38255	38355	38155
378256	38056	38256	38356	38156
378257	38057	38257	38357	38157

(d)   Fitted with de-icing equipment

[1] – Named *Professor Sir Peter Hall*
[2] – Named *Ian Brown CBE*

LEA VALLEY AND ROMFORD – UPMINSTER LINES
CLASS 315

UNIT No.	DMSO	MSO	PTSO	DMSO
31501	64461	71281	71389	64462
31502	64463	71282	713920	64464
31503	64465	71283	71391	64466
31504	64467	71284	71392	64468
31505	64469	71285	71393	64470
31506	64471	71286	71394	64472
31507	64473	71287	71395	64474
31508	64475	71288	71396	64476
31509	64477	71289	71397	64478
31510	64479	71290	71398	64480
31511	64481	71291	71399	64482
31512	64483	71292	71400	64484
31513	64485	71293	71401	64486
31514	64487	71294	71402	64488
31515	64489	71295	71403	64490
31516	64491	71296	71404	64492
31517[1]	64493	71297	71405	64494

1 - Named *Transport for London*

CLASS 317/7

UNIT No.	DTSO	MSO	TSO	DTCO
317708	77007	62668	71584	77055
317709	77008	62669	71585	77056
317710	77009	62670	71586	77057
317714	77013	62674	71590	77061
317719	77018	62679	71595	77066
317723	77022	62683	71599	77070
317729	77038	62689	71605	77076
317732	77031	62692	71608	77079

CLASS 317/8

UNIT No.	DTSO	MSO	TCO	DTSO
317887	77043	62707	71606	77077
317888	77030	62691	71607	77078
317889	77032	62693	71609	77080
317890	77033	62694	71610	77081
317892	77034	62695	71611	77082
317892[1]	77035	62696	71612	77083

[1] – Named *Ilford Depot*

CLASS 710/1 – AC

UNIT No.	TBA	TBA	TBA	TBA
710101	431101	431401	431301	431501
710102	431102	434102	431302	431502
710103	431103	431403	431303	431503
710104	431104	431404	431304	431504
710105	431105	431405	431305	431505
710106	431106	431406	431306	431506
710107	431107	431407	431307	431507
710108	431108	431408	431308	431508
710109	431109	431409	431309	431509
710110	431110	431410	431310	431510
710111	431111	431411	431311	431511
710112	431112	431412	431312	431512
710113	431113	431413	431313	431513
710114	431114	431414	431314	431514
710115	431115	431415	431315	431515
710116	431116	431416	431316	431516
710117	431117	431417	431317	431517
710118	431118	431418	431318	431518
710119	431119	431419	431319	431519
710120	431120	431420	431320	431520
710121	431121	431421	431321	431521
710122	431122	431422	431322	431522
710123	431123	431423	431323	431523
710124	431124	431424	431324	431524
710125	431125	431425	431325	431525
710126	431126	431426	431326	431526
710127	431127	431427	431327	431527
710128	431128	431428	431328	431528
710129	431129	431429	431329	431529
710130	431130	431430	431330	431530
710131	431131	431431	431331	431531

GOSPEL OAK – BARKING AND WATFORD DC LINES

Class 710/2 – AC/DC

UNIT No.	TBA	TBA	TBA	TBA
710256	432156	432456	432356	432556
710257	432157	432457	432357	432557
710258	432158	432458	432358	432558
710259	432159	432459	432359	432559
710260	432160	432460	432360	432560
710261	432161	432461	432361	432561
710262	432162	432462	432362	432562
710263	432163	432463	432363	432563
710264	432164	432464	432364	432564
710265	432165	432465	432365	432565
710266	432166	432466	432366	432566
710267	432167	432467	432367	432567
710268	432168	432468	432368	432568
710269	432169	432469	432369	432569

TFL RAIL

LIVERPOOL STREET TO SHENFIELD

CLASS 315

UNIT No.	DMSO	TSO	PTSO	DMSO
315818	64495	71298	71406	64496
315819	64497	71299	71407	64498
315820	64499	71300	71408	64500
315821	64501	71301	71409	64502
315822	64503	71302	71410	64504
315823	64505	71303	71411	64506
315824	64507	71304	71412	64508
315825	64509	71305	71413	64510
315826	64511	71206	71414	64512
315827	64513	71207	71415	64514
315828	64515	71308	71416	64516
315829[1]	64517	71309	71417	64518
315830	64519	71310	71418	64520
315831	64521	71311	71419	64522
315832	64523	71312	71420	64524
315833	64525	71313	71421	64526
315834	64527	71314	71422	64528
315835	64529	71315	71423	64530
315836	64531	71316	71424	64532
315837	64533	71317	71425	64534
315838	64535	71318	71426	64536
315839	64537	71319	71427	64538
315840	64539	71320	71428	64540
315841	64541	71321	71429	64542
315842	64543	71322	71430	64544
315843	64545	71323	71431	64546
315844	64547	71324	71432	64548
315845[2]	64549	71325	71433	64550
315846	64551	71326	71434	64552
315847	64553	71327	71435	64554
315848	64555	71328	71436	64556
315849	64557	71329	71437	64558
315850	64559	71330	71438	64560
315851	64561	71331	71439	64562
315852	64563	71332	71440	64564
315853	64565	71333	71441	64566
315854	64567	71334	71442	64568
315855	64569	71335	71443	64570
315856	64571	71336	71444	64572
315857	64573	71337	71445	64574
315858	64575	71338	71446	64576
315859	64577	71339	71447	64578
315860	64579	71340	71448	64580
315861	64581	71341	71449	64582

[1] - Named *London Borough of Havering Celebrating 40 Years*
[2] - Named *Herbie Woodward*

CROSSRAIL — ELIZABETH LINE

CLASS 345/0

UNIT No.	DMSO(A)	PMSO(A)	MSO(A)	MSO(B)	TSO	MSO(C)	MSO(D)	PMSO(B)	DMSO(B)
345001	340101	340201	340301	340401*	340501	340601*	340701	340801	340901
345002	340102	340201	340302	340402*	340502	340602*	340702	340802	340902
345003	340103	340203	340303	340403*	340503	340603*	340703	340803	340903
345004	340104	340204	340304	340404*	340504	340604*	340704	340804	340904
345005	340105	340205	340305	340405*	340505	340605*	340705	340805	340905
345006	340106	340206	340306	340406*	340506	340606*	340706	340806	340906
345007	340107	340207	340307	340407*	340507	340607*	340707	340807	340907
345008	340108	340208	340308	340408*	340508	340608*	340708	340808	340908
345009	340109	340209	340309	340409*	340509	340609*	340709	340809	340909
345010	340110	340210	340310	340410*	340510	340610*	340710	340810	340910
345011	340111	340211	340311	340411*	340511	340611*	340711	340811	340911
345012	340112	340212	340312	340412*	340512	340612*	340712	340812	340912
345013	340113	340213	340313	340413*	340513	340613*	340713	340813	340913
345014	340114	340214	340314	340414*	340514	340614*	340714	340814	340914
345015	340115	340215	340315	340415*	340515	340615*	340715	340815	340915
345016	340116	340216	340316	340416	340516	340616	340716	340816	340916
345017	340117	340217	340317	340417	340517	340617	340717	340817	340917
345018	340118	340218	340318	340418	340518	340618	340718	340818	340918
345019	340119	340219	340319	340419	340519	340619	340719	340819	340919
345020	340120	340220	340320	340420	340520	340620	340720	340820	340920
345021	340121	340221	340321	340421	340521	340621	340721	340821	340921
345022	340122	340222	340322	340422	340522	340622	340722	340822	340922
345023	340123	340223	340323	340423	340523	340623	340723	340823	340923
345024	340124	340224	340324	340424	340524	340624	340724	340824	340924
345025	340125	340225	340325	340425	340525	340625	340725	340825	340925
345026	340126	340226	340326	340426	340526	340626	340726	340826	340926
345027	340127	340227	340327	340427	340527	340627	340727	340827	340927
345028	340128	340228	340328	340428	340528	340628	340728	340828	340928
345029	340129	340229	340329	340429	340529	340629	340729	340829	340929
345030	340130	340230	340330	340430	340530	340630	340730	340830	340930
345031	340131	340231	340331	340431	340531	340631	340731	340831	340931
345032	340132	340232	340332	340432	340532	340632	340732	340832	340932
345033	340133	340233	340333	340433	340533	340633	340733	340833	340933
345034	340134	340234	340334	340434	340534	340634	340734	340834	340934
345025	340135	340235	340335	340435	340535	340635	340735	340835	340935
345026	340136	340236	340336	340436	340536	340636	340736	340836	340936
345037	340137	340237	340337	340437	340537	340637	340737	340837	340937
345038	340138	340238	340338	340438	340538	340638	340738	340838	340938
345039	340139	340239	340339	340439	340539	340639	340739	340839	340939
345040	340140	340240	343340	340440	340540	340640	340740	340840	340940
345041	340141	340241	340341	340441	340541	340641	340741	340841	340941
345042	340142	340242	340342	340442	340542	340642	340742	340842	340942
345043	340143	340243	340343	340443	340543	340643	340743	340843	340943
345044	340144	340244	340344	340444	340544	340644	340744	340844	340944
345045	340145	340245	340345	340445	340545	340645	340745	340845	340945
345046	340146	340246	340346	340446	340546	340646	340746	340846	340946
345047	340147	340247	340347	340447	340547	340647	340747	340847	340947
345048	340148	340248	340348	340448	340548	340648	340748	340848	340948
345049	340149	340249	340349	340449	340549	340649	340749	340849	340949

*MSO car initially omitted from the formation to allow 7-car operation between Liverpool Street and Shenfield. Trains between Paddington and Heathrow Airport will be introduced as full 9-car trains and all Class 345s will be so-formed by the end of 2019.